FROM FAITH TO FAITH

Poetic Fragments for a Theology

ALSO BY RIC COUCHMAN

Musings from Outside the Universal

A Famine of Tears

Blueprint for a Nihilism

Conflagration of Ouranos

3:00 A.M.

Following the Blue Morpho

The Little Boy from Water Street

FROM FAITH TO FAITH

Poetic Fragments for a Theology

RIC COUCHMAN

WITH A FOREWORD

BY

"TWO LITTLE FRIENDS IN A GARDEN"

A WAN WAN DUTTY BOOK

WAN WAN DUTTY

Book design and cover by Ric Couchman

Printed in the United States of America

ISBN 979-8-234-05251-3

HONORING

THE

MEMORY

OF

MIRIAM

(My Dearest Friend)

&

ALSO

MICHAEL

BERTRAND

&

REMA

"My Eternal Father, it appears that Your Chosen, Your favored ones from the west of Asia continue to take a page (I Samuel 15:3) on prosecuting war (with impunity) out of your Holy playBook. Like Father like Chosen I guess."

Andreas Pistis

CONTENTS

FOREWORD
by
Two Little Friends in a Garden

"What is he doing now, Bede?"

"He is kneeling on the ground. Looks like he is praying. Let's move in closer. Here. Take my hand. I will lead you. Let's stop here. This is a good spot."

"Are the twelve with him?"

"No. I believe he left them sleeping near the garden gate."

"Should we go to him now and ask him? I am scared. What if he says, 'No'."

"Let's wait until he is done praying. As soon as he is done we will go to him. And I don't think he will say, no. Remember what he said the last time we saw him speaking to the crowd?"

"I don't remember. Remind me."

"He said, 'Allow little children to come unto me, and do not forbid them, for of such is the kingdom of heaven.'"

"Ah...I remember now."

"Wow!..."

"What?...What is happening, Bede?"

"Shhh....Not so loud. He will hear us. Wow! He is sweating quite a lot...It looks like blood... I wonder if he is hurt...This is unbelievable! He is sweating blood."

"Oh my! Should we go help him? Let's go help him."

"Wait...He is still praying...Oh, no! Would you believe it!? He is saying he no longer wants to go through with the task God gave him. He can't do that!!!! He has to stay the course. He is pleading with God and asking God's permission to not continue with his task. How can he? How can he give up now?"

"Oh, no!!!! We've got to stop him from quitting, Bede. Let's go tell him that he can't give up now. If he gives up now he won't be able to make me see. I don't want to be blind anymore."

"O, Carlos, don't cry. Let's kneel in prayer together and ask God to give him strength to complete his mission. You pray first."

"Okay. Dear God, please give Mr. Hay-sus the strength and courage to complete the job you sent him on earth to do…Amen. Oh, and dear God, so he can do a miracle for me and make me able to see."

"Yes, dear God. He cannot give up now. Please, Please don't let him give up now. Please give him courage and strength to complete his mission. He cannot throw in the towel now. All of humanity is relying on him…Carlos is relying on him."

PREFACE

No one has made a more lasting impression on me than did Andreas Pistis. Who is Andreas Pistis, you might ask? The truth is I never met him. Everything I know about him I heard from my dear friend, Father Ionnes Klimakos, who first met him in a confession booth. And thereafter they became very close. Describing that first encounter, Father Klimakos said, "I smelled him before I heard his Bless-me-Father-for-I-have-sinned greeting. I almost fainted from the smell. It was the overpowering odor of his unwashed body and clothing, and the combined smell of urine, fecal matter, and sweaty, socked feet that never saw the light of day."

Father Ionnes decribed Andreas Pistis as having slightly sunken cheeks, a bronze complexion, a straight back, a Zen-like aspect, and a white, Castro-like beard that gave him the appearance of a rebel sage. "There was something compelling about him," he said. "And his eyes...his eyes seemed to emit a certain power and confidence, though with a hint of sadness. One eye glittered, only one, like our Ancient Mariner's." And I remember quipping, "Did he have an albatross around his neck?" To which Father Ionnes did not respond, and he did not appear to find my remark funny.

From my many conversations and written correspondences about Andreas Pistis with Father

Ionnes, it was apparent that something about the man tugged at his spirit, such that he would often come away from their meetings with, as he put it, 'the Mount Sainai glow.' That came as no surprise to me, for I was myself captivated by Father Ionnes's recounting of that which Andreas Pistis shared with him over the course of their all too brief but quite substantive relationship, with Father Ionnes never seeing or hearing from him again and concluding that he had no doubt gone off into the woods to transition out of his "existence cycle" as he always told him he would do when he felt his time drawing to a close.

What does Andreas Pistis have to do with this book? Well, it reflects his mind, his spirit, his heart, but most importantly it represents a literary sculpture of his person, my interpretation and filtering of Father Ionnes's account. It is a literary construction entirely of my making - employing my passion, my imagination, and my artistic gift – a construction no less substantive than the man to whom Father Ionnes introduced me.

I pondered long and hard on the medium through which to give Andrea Pistis expression. I could not present him in sonorous chronological prose narrative. He can only be presented artistically, poetically. And so I offer him here in lyrical and narrative poetic fragments, unshackling him from particulars and universals and giving him transcendence and freedom within the imagination.

What these poetic fragments illustrate is the evolution of Andreas Pistis's faith experience as he navigated life's landscape, as well and his various transitions within this faith experience. From the things he shared with Father Ionnes and from the manner in which he articulated them, it appeared obvious to me that Andreas Pistis was not interested in articulating universal principles or categorical imperatives. He cared little for dogma and systematic theology. His primary objective was to make sense of his own existence and to navigate his existence in a manner that functioned effectively for him. And to the extent that a Theology emerged from his experience, that Theology was not a corollary of his experience. It evolved in his experience and simultaneously became the undercurrent of his experience. Moreover, his emergent theology was no categorical imperative for humanity, only for himself. He would not dare will that his theology become universal law. His theology was for him only; it was simply his "flip-flops with which to navigate the rainforest" – to navigate his existence landscape, not for anyone else.

Andreas Pistis's singular focus throughout his faith odyssey seemed to be his relationship with his Eternal Father and redefining that relationship in a way that made sense to him. God was for him his

Father, nothing more, and with Whom he could experience all the ideals in a father-son relationship he himself never had. And at the foundation of that relationship was the Incarnation - a topic that was very dear to his heart according to Father Ionnes. He told Father Ionnes that an Incarnation in which Jesus is both God and Man "in some ridiculously hybrid arrangement wherein He could fall back on His deity should the sh*t hit the fan" did not work for him or capture his childlike imagination. But an Incarnation in which God freely and absolutely gave up His deity, risking His deity to become human in order to liberate humanity, stirred his sensibilities, stoked his imagination, solidified his confidence in humanity, and sealed in his mind that God now knows him, now understands him, and is now accessible to him by virtue of His Incarnation.

But just as important was the new mindset Andreas Pistis incorporated in his redefining his relationship with his Father – fear and trembling. Not fear of God in the sense of being afraid of Him, but the realization that God as his Eternal Father and with Whom he shared a unique relationship is also Father to each of his fellow humans who also (in principle) enjoy a unique relationship with the Father and that they are equally as precious in God's eyes as he (Andreas) is in His. That understanding made his fellow humans sacred in his eyes. He saw himself in others and others in himself, thus influencing the manner in which he related to them, such that "to help one human was to help all humanity" – a concept he learned from Islam.

As I conclude this note, I wish to point out the following: First, a word about the primary title, *From Faith to Faith.* The phrase (taken from Romans, Chapter 1 verse 17) has been the topic of much debate among exegetes. I have no interest in speculating on its contextual meaning but have used it here in the sense of organic transitions in the faith experience without regard to quantity or quality.

Secondly, this book is no recommendation of Andreas Pistis or of his mindset. It simply celebrates a rebel, albeit a flawed one, who accepted the status quo and who was unafraid to critique aspects of it. "I am a Hindu at heart," Father Ionnes recalled him fervently declaring, "but I am fiercely Christian. Christianity was functional for me at a very critical juncture of my life, and I would defend it to the hilt. That does not mean it is impervious to my critique. Absolutely not. I will critique it as necessary but strictly in the context of my relationship with my Eternal Father...and always with fear and trembling."

Lastly, the poetic fragments that follow are not organized in any uniform manner by themes, subject matter, chronology, etc. They are loosely arranged (somewhat like the aphoristic forms of Pascal, Voltaire, and Nietzsche), reflecting the complex and the simple, the amorphous and the coherent, and the spirit and its human experience. And if the reader looks to specifically identify Andreas Pistis in the various fragments, she will invariably not find such direct identification as the speaker's perspective might be that of a male or female adult or a male of female child, and with fleeting glimpses of Andreas here and there. But the reader can rest assured that he is there. If not in form or character, he is there in the action and thoughts of the various "speakers" in the fragments. His spirit pervades the Poetic Fragments as they spotlight, as I imagined it, his odyssey From Faith to Faith.

FROM FAITH TO FAITH

Poetic Fragments for a Theology

"When I was a child
I thought like a child..."

Christus Victor

"So,...
He descended into Hell.
Now, what?"

"Just wait.
You ain't seen nothing yet;
The best is yet to come."

On the Existence of God

I find it difficult to understand
How someone as smart as you
Could believe in God's existence.
There is no God.

Smart I am not,
Wise maybe,
But not smart.
I would be dumb to deny God's existence.
My very existence presupposes His.

If there is no God,
There is no I.
I am because He exists.
I exist,
Therefore, God exists.
And if in affirming God's existence
I am presumed dumb,
Then I proudly wear the name tag.

From Faith to Faith

"Like a Tree"

Ask the little child.
Raise the question
Of her misplaced faith
As she kneels expectant,
Imploring Saint Peter
To remove the pain.
Tell her about her self-deceit
Deplore her lack of reason.

Proclaim to the nineteen-year-old
His deluded and enslaved mind
Because thanksgiving he gives
To his Jehovah-Jireh
For the cassava porridge--
Barely enough,
Laid out carefully in five plates
Before five hungry mouths.

Chide the husband for daring to believe,
For ingesting *the opiate of the people*
(Feurbach's phrase)
As he waits hours before the flight
For confirmation of the ticket's purchase,
Not knowing from whence the funds
Would come to ensure
His and his family's transportation.

Berate his ignorance, as you deem it.
Refute the embattled mother
As she agonizes over her ailing child
Lying in bed consumed by fiery fever
And as she pleads with her God,
Begging that He would show mercy.
Contradict her belief in God's imminence.
Demolish her premise of faith.
Tell her that her hope is in vain.

Hear their response, O erudite one.
Consider their resilience of faith
Despite your attempt to subvert their faith.
Consider their refusal to capitulate.
Note their resolve to stay steadfast.
And if in the end they are proved wrong,
Observe their satisfaction in thinking
That their faith was still worth it after all.

"Take Away the Stone"

And when I heard that you had left,
I went into my office, and I wept.

Our friend, [Bertrand] has fallen asleep.

Did you depart on your own terms?
For it appears you were so inclined;
At least, such was my impression
Based on our recent conversation.
But it feels like it was only yesterday
That I heard you say:

"I was a quiet guy who never fought back;
And oh! How I do regret that."

Those were your parting words to me.
And I, since, did not reach out to you,
And oh! How I do regret that.

Lord, the one whom you love is sick.

And the winter season is upon safari land,
And your Rosa's womb has seen only winter
And twice failed to bear the expected fruit.
I'm so sorry; pardon my assumption.
Indeed, you were not as bold as we,

Forthright with the women, assertive.
With that observation I surely agree,
But depressed like Michael Earle?
With that comparison I do not concur.
Shy you were, no doubt, and timid,
But you possessed a solidity and depth;
Perhaps, that was why I sorely wept.

How painful must have been the absence
Of that strong male voice deep within
Which ideally should have been your father's,
He whom you said you loved yet hated
Because you could not measure up–
Measure up to his standards of manliness:

"I struggled with a weakness, privately...,
I guess you must have suspected..."

Ah...the shame and guilt of Christianity.

"...Being made to feel like a leper,
The intense shame, the inner turmoil,
All because, as they would say
(If with Paul you do agree),
God gave me over to a reprobate mind.
But what do they know?
They know nought about me."

That healing you sought never came,
That desire to be fully known, warts and all,
To be fully accepted and embraced truly...
And then your question about Joi's sexuality...
And in that question you revealed
The true nature of your struggle and ordeal.

Take away the stone.

My question at first you evaded,
But you subsequently affirmed the struggle.
A glimpse of those thoughts of ending all
You gave to me, and of your inner shame,
And of how dark a time it was for you –
No more handshakes, no more embrace,
Greeted, yes, but not touched, you said,
Rejected by [y]our Bible-toting friends.

And your Rosa knew,
Faithful Rosa who stood by you.
But you continued to honor your marital vow;
You honored it to the end...
As with the struggle within you did contend.
And your animated and vigorous response:

"Yes! Yes! That's it! That's it!

It has indeed been a living hell!"

Jesus wept.

A living hell it was for you, you said,
And so you took your leave, abruptly,
As was your custom back then,
When without warning
You would leave our conversations.
In like manner you abruptly departed,
Leaving this self-absorbed, insensitive world
That pays lip-service to righteousness and piety
But is entirely vacuous regarding compassion,
Leaving the Conversation and your Opposers
To find and enjoy elsewhere
The peace that was denied you here—
In this life--
Where it mattered most.

Shantih, Shantih, Shantih

In Search of Paradise

S.L., may sleep be kind to you this night.

Three succinct points made about the dead
And then a few beers after, to catch up,
To reminisce on the good times past.
Are the dead not worthy?
Are they not allowed in our memories?
And talking about the dead,
There was one standing right there,
Stunningly beautiful,
Contemplative, wistful,
Longing, perhaps, for that lost paradise,
Offering a good first impression,
Blowing smoke into the cold night air,
And rising up like a Phoenix
From the ashes scattered at her feet.
But first impressions evaporate in smoke,
As between confidence and cigarettes
There exists a tenuous connection.
(That's what my mom used to say).
What was her name again?
It was forgotten in meaningless talk,
In between rounds of beer and wine.
And for some unknown reason that night
I temporarily chased away Mr. Hyde,
Shaking off the predator instinct,

That primal, baser aspect.
Then from my mouth these words,
"Do not drink anymore; have some water."
And staring intently at my face she asked,
"Who are you?"
With emphasis on "are"
This was not what she expected,
This was not what she was used to,
It was not the customary come-on.
And for the tenth time she escaped,
Seeking refuge in a cigarette,
Then returning to the bar
And for the tenth time asked, "Who are you?"
This time with tears in her eyes.
Why was she there?
Why was I there?
Were we there because of that endless search,
That enervating search for the paradise we lost?
And the tears streamed down her face,
And again her question, "Who are you?"
How many times?
I had lost count.
And this time I answered,
"I am an angel sent to guide you.
May you find the paradise you lost."
What moved me to speak those words to her?

I have no answer,
But I truly meant them.
And I turned,
And walked out of the bar,
Walked out into the cold night,
In search of the paradise I had lost,
To return to the paradise I had lost,
Regretful of the paradise I had lost.

My Miriam

I have stopped asking Him for anything;
He has to make things so complicated.
If I ask for paper He'll give me a tree.
If I ask for money for my airfare,
He'll give it to me at the last minute.
And then I'm told by my friends
He is teaching me patience,
And that He know what's best
And all the usual Christian-speak.
I never know if His answer is Yes or No.
He doesn't even acknowledge when I ask.
When I prayed for Him to heal my grandma,
Guess what he did?
He took her away.
I get more stressed awaiting His answers,
And by the time He gives what I ask for,
I am too emotionally spent to enjoy it.
You ask and plead with Him for something,
And what does He do?
He becomes a schoolteacher -
Teaches you lessons.
(And those friends of mine again...
Why don't they just shut up.)
I have decided to stop going to Him
Whenever I am in need of anything.
And do you know what?

From Faith to Faith

You won't believe it!
Because of that I am spared those lessons,
Like lessons in patience.
It's always patience.
(Do you hear those friends again?)
Instead, I am going to the Immaculate One.
She is a hell of a lot more understanding.
She really listens to me,
And she always has that kind, gentle look.
You know what I just thought of?
If my grandma were here
And I had asked for that airfare,
She would have given it in a heartbeat
Without the muteness,
Without the lessons,
Without the interminable waiting,
Without the serious looking face,
(He ought to shave off that beard)
And all that stuff.
I really do miss grandma,
But then, I do have my dearest Miriam.
"...pray for us, sinners,
Now and at the hour of our death. Amen."

Portrait of the Poet as a Christian

This know, my friend, that I am a synthesis,
A synthesis of congruence and contradiction.
To Life, with all its nuances,
I open my arms.
I laugh, I live, I love.
Nature is my Playground,
My Inspiration,
My Sustenance,
My Source.
Freedom, creativity, and thought,
I hold sacred.
With Gods and…
Do not interrupt me!…
With Gods and Religion, I co-exist.
Humanity is the only dogma I accept.
Life and people make sense.
Injustice, violence, and oppression I abhor,
And that Man's agenda on behalf of
The poor, the captives, the blind,
And those who are oppressed,
I endorse and undertake.
I respect tradition, norms, and customs,
But their imposition, I resist.
Contradiction and Congruence
I embrace.
I am a Rebel who follows the rules.

From Faith to Faith

Behind the Closed Door

Behind that door
A conversation ensues -
A unilateral dialogue
If I may say so,
A misnomer that phrase
Since in a dialogue
Two are necessary.
At your own risk
You enter, I dare say.
And if enter you do,
Full responsibility
Falls squarely on you
For that which is heard.
And what you do with it
Is entirely up to you.
Weigh carefully your choice.
My suggestion is that you do not enter -
A question of lost innocence?
But if you do enter,
You are committed;
There is no turning back.
Wait…there is one last thing…
Everything you hear in there
Stays behind that door.
You may enter now

"…not always like this.
Yesterday, I saw something…
One moment please…

So you chose to enter, stranger(s)?
Please make yourself comfortable.

…As I was saying…
I saw something yesterday – an immolation,
Made me sick to my stomach.
Shit like this happens every day.
Violence and injustice everywhere,
The poor raped and plundered,
The middle class, disappearing.
How do yoU expect me to see this shit
And be normal again?
How do yoU expect me to live
Amongst such interminable suffering?
Do yoU expect us to remain human still?
The image of that little girl,
Trapped for sixty hours,
Cold, frightened, shivering,
Trapped in the volcanic debris,
Has never left me.
Her innocent, glassy eyes still follow me.
I hear that shot also,

The one that took the life
Of that young Vietnamese.
I smell the stench of the dead at Bashir
And feel the gaze of those staring
Through barbed wire, emaciated, dead,
Awaiting the fumes of the gas chamber.
Shall I go on?
I see visual images of it,
Read it in print,
Hear about it sometimes,
And on rear occasions, experience it first-hand.
And yoU put the blame on us!
Are you out of youR fucking minD
This fucked up world is youR world.
YoU brought about this mess.
And yoU dare to hold us responsible!?
To hold me responsible!?
What the fuck is wrong with yoU?
Talking about us falling short?
About us being depraved and deceitful?
Try living in this world and see what happens.
Who would be the same
After living in and seeing this shit?
All this is youR doing;
yoU are looking for scapegoats
To blame for youR fuck-up.

All have sinned? The sin is entirely yourS.
Either do something about youR problem
Or leave us the fuck alone.
yoU love to put us on a guilt trip,
To make us feel like we are the worst.
yoU are the guilty onE!
yoU alone are culpable.
I have never killed anyone.
yoU have slaughtered countless numbers -
Babies, children, men, women.
It's all there in youR play Book.
The man with the beard and long blonde hair,
Him I can stand, but boy do I hate yoU.
Yes, I hate yoU
Because of how you made me feel as a child.
All that fear I carried around in me,
Fear of burning in hell - And for what?
For drinking the condensed milk?
For telling a harmless, little lie to my friends?
No child should have to carry such fear.
And yoU did nothing to remove it.
All the prayers I made
Which yoU never answered,
Making me think it was that I was a bad boy
And not worthy.
All my friends taken away in childhood,

What kind of goD are yoU?
What kind of goD does this stuff?
Sometimes I think you are the wizarD -
You know...like the wizard of Oz.
Some small old man who wants to act big.
I think you are jealous of your creation;
YoU wish yoU could fuck and eat like we.
Putting the blame on us....
Why do yoU just stand there? Or sit there?
Whatever it is yoU do...
Why don't yoU say something?
As usual, you have nothing to say.
And I still think of those days in my childhood,
The days yoU did nothing
Dispite all my tears and my pleas.
I begged, and I begged, and I begged,
Begged yoU to make it stop
My only hope was yoU
To deliver me from the torment and torrent
Of repulsive gropings, kisses, and penetrations
(By the one who sired me, the one I call...father)
And from the endless pain in that part of my body
That I hate – that revolting part between my legs,
And worst, with my mother near yet distant,
Perhaps too embarrassed at my shame and hers,
And voiding contact with me eye to eye.

So here I kneel in the suppliant's posture,
Broken and beaten from the assaults
Of all those men who claim to love me
But never stayed.
Here I prostrate myself again before you,
Worn out from childbearing
And besieged and ravaged by old age.
And as in all the years past,
I know the response – silence.
And yet I come,
Day after day pouring out my soul,
But I will say that which many desire to say
But are muted by fear.
I fear yoU not,
For you cannot torment me more
Than that which I have already suffered.
No worse can you do;
For, youR Hell pales in comparison.
And I so want to say..."Screw yoU!"
I want to hate You,
But I can't.
I do not know how.
Deep inside I know You are my only hope.
You are the only One upon Whom I can dump,
Upon Whom I can dump my anger and hate.
My Safe Place is You,

And I thank You.
I thank You for being my Safe Place
Upon Whom to rest my emotions.
Amen.

"Thank you for coming in, stranger(s),
For sharing in my pain and suffering.
Treat my jewels with respect, please.
That's all I ask of you.
And as you leave,
Please close the door behind you."

Ma'm/Sir, Walk this way, please.
And do be mindful of that which I said
Before you entered that sad space:
Everything you heard in that room
Stays in that room.

The Red Shoes

"The one in white is not necessarily the one who is pure and not necessarily the one who is holy."
--Sabio

And I am liberated,
The transformation complete,
With just that final thrust of my feet
Into that pair of unmitigated acceptance.
This evolution!
This transportation!
This soaring upwards!
This emancipation
Of the woman in me.
A vanquishing for the moment only,
But a triumph still.
Tall and proud I sprout,
And elegant too,
And growing more and more confident
With every beat of that tantalizingly rhythmic
Clop, clop, clop I hear
As I walk a gauntlet of gawkers not a few.
Aware of the stares,
Of the heads that are turned,
Not from the longings of the loins,
Nor from seeing "the woman,"
For of her they have no sight

Because blinded by bias, and intolerance,
Choosing instead to see
The one from whom I flee,
The 'man' from whom I long to escape,
The 'man' with whom I am forever bound.
But I hear that clop, clop, clop,
And remember I am "woman,"
I feel "woman,"
Tall, elegant, and free.

And there, there it is - that extra spring.
I feel that extra spring in my gait
As I sashay along that gauntlet of hate
Through the giggles and through the disdain.
And refusing to let my spirit wane,
I lose myself in that clop, clop of freedom,
Rising up like an unyielding trunk
Out of sanguine roots of passion,
Losing myself in my pair of symbols of peace
From which my 'feminine' springs.

And the derision hangs in the air,
But the derision bothers me not,
For by an impervious vision protected.
My vision is of the adulation,
Of the awakened desires,

And of the flattering catcalls --
A vision created in my imagination
To erase the pain.
I remain numb to the hate and insults,
Even to those I receive within my own *ekklesia.*
For I am bouyed by the power of knowing
I live and move and have my being in Him
Whose peace surrounds me,
Whose grace sustains me,
And whose love comforts me.
Because of that I embrace my true self.
Because of that I embrace my freedom to be.
And because of that I embrace the woman in me.

And the clop, clop echoes,
And the clop, clop fades,
Taking with it exaggerated motions
Of shoulders and hips and head.
And later the "woman," too, will recede,
Pulled back into this onerous trap,
Into this male body He gave me,
And with nowhere else to go.
And the closet door will hide the red pair
Until they are brought forth once again,
Called into service once more
To liberate me from my body's torment

And to release me,
The real me –
The "Woman" in me –
To release the "Woman" in me.

Late Comes the Dawn

A fleeting moment's enjoyment,
But it was a thought quickly extirpated,
Denied, thrust out of mind,
With perhaps a willingness
To entertain that it was nothing
But a creation of the imagination,
A disgusting and despicable way of being,
Unsupported by tradition,
Castigated by religious injunction,
Its once lofty position among the Greeks lost,
And to Gomorrah's sanction relegated.

Close friends they were, these two
(Like Patroclus and Achilleus),
In the fullness of their youth,
Both serving His cause.
Anointed with His Spirit were they,
And on a mission most sacred--
"To preach good news to the poor,
To proclaim release to the captives,
And recovering of sight to the blind,
To set at liberty those who are oppressed,
To proclaim the acceptable year of the Lord."
Andreas the younger,
And Petros the older but not by much.

And with the world before them
Awaiting their exploits,
Andreas saw in the other
The consummate object of emulation,
The brother he did not have.
The other, the older,
In profound esteem the younger held,
Like David's love for a younger Jonathan.

On that fateful day
At the time when cocks celebrate
The breaking of dawn
And kiskadees hail the rising sun,
That friendship was slain,
Unwittingly killed by desire,
An innocuous movement of the hand
Making contact with warm flesh,
And Eros is stirred.
Not fully released from sleep's prison
The other reciprocates,
Hand searching, finding, stroking.
Two friends, close friends,
Hovering between sleep and wakefulness,
In an instant,
But in what seemed an eternity,
Caught in a moment of innocent discovery.

And what a discovery for the younger!
That he for his kind this fleeting desire had,
Finding pleasure in his own reciprocation,
Raising in his mind the horrifying query
Whether he were of that kind -
Of those "*given over to a reprobate mind,*
Participating in the unseemingly."-
A thing unthinkable that such a thought
Should his mind pervade
Or in his mind find momentary reception.

In that instant hate filled his racing heart,
Overthrowing reason and insight,
And forcing a wedge between friendship.
From that moment the younger withdrew,
In his mind blaming the older for the event,
Refusing to accept
That fleeting moment of desire
For his own kind
And fearing, utterly fearing,
The compromise of his manhood.

Concerning that singular episode
The two friends exchanged not a word,
But tension filled the air.
A dark cloud hung over them.

For his part the older reached out still,
For he truly loved the younger.
But that fiery-hearted young soul
Would have no part of it,
Feeling let down and betrayed
By him whom he deemed his
Mentor, brother, confidante, friend.

Much wiser with the passing of years,
Andreas looked back with sadness,
No longer holding the older culpable,
But long since coming to terms
With the reality of the human contradiction
And accepting the complexities of humanness.
Disdaining absolutes,
Especially those that abrogate empathy,
He judged no one,
A line that, in fear and trembling,
He refused to cross,
Remaining respectful of tradition's censorship,
And of his Heavenly Father's sanctions
But refusing to accept their dictates.

Much older and wiser with the passing years,
He longed to see his friend again
From whom long since separated,

And Imagining a possible meeting
And the words he would say
If face to face they met again:
"I understand, Petros.
I truly understand."

Wondering Whether

Those six years of his youth,
Between eighteen and twenty-three,
Exchanged for custody of four,
Not by choice but by design,
As if destiny and chance colluded
In some clandestine plot
To make alterations to the sequence,
Prematurely depositing him...,
In fact, more like a dumping...
Dumping him into responsibility.
No one bothered to consult him.
Neither did You-Know-Who consult him,
But he accepted without protestation,
Going along with His plan,
Giving no thought to the sacrifice.
And though nursing some bitterness within,
He did that which he was asked to do
For the sake of those four of his blood.
Such was his essence.
He could not do otherwise.
His nature did not permit him.
And through those years,
Mustering all the strength that lay within,
He carried them.
Though often worn out and tired,
He carried them--

Instilling in them hope,
Teaching them contentment and fortitude,
Leading them by example.
They looked to him as parent and big brother.
They looked to him as teacher and provider.
He guided them through times of hardship,
And those were many.
He led them through times of happiness,
And those were few.
So yes, he carried them,
But the Almighty carried him.
He exchanged his weakness for God's strength.
On account of His strength he carried them.
He carried them without weariness
And carried them without fainting.

There were times when he was bitter,
Bitter on account of his incompleteness–
About missing that critical period of his youth,
Though exceedingly wiser for the experience.
And in those moments when he wondered
After all these years
Whether bitter or thankful he should be,
He was quite clear as to the answer.

Nazarite Vow

Where the shadows walk
In between life and death
I refused the hand offered--
A gesture of truce,
An invitation to servitude,
But on that Fallen Star
My back I turned.

Where darkness broods
In between being and nothingness
I kissed the hands offered.
I held them firmly,
Two pierced hands
Offering freedom from bondage.
I embraced the bright, morning star.

Descarrego

om shantih, shantih, shantih
in nomine Patris, et Filii, et Spiritūs Sancti…

Ruler of the world, Sovereign supreme
Before anything was formed,
My almighty, my all powerful Orixas -
Olodumare, Olorun, Olofi -
I worship You.

Most Gracious, Most Merciful God,
Our Mother, our Father, Jah Rastafari,
Oneness of Life and Light
And Greatest of all,
We praise You -
You Who are our fragrance,
Our *Banho de Folhas,*
And Who nourish well all beings.
There is none but You.
You generated us.
You gave birth to us.
You feed us from Your breasts.
You deliver us from afflictions.
You are our living YHWH who saves,
Our Rock when grief or trials befall.

Show me the straight path,

O Mistress of the Day of Judgment.
Show me the path of those
Whom You have favored,
Not the path of those who go astray.
For the sake of immortality
Liberate me from death.
Help me shed the foolishness within.
Calm my anxious and chaotic mind.
Give peace to my ravaged psyche,
And transform me into a conduit of Love.

Holy One, trusting in your Great Compassion,
We empty ourselves before You
So that Your Spirit may fill and control us,
For in your power only, we find our strength.
Amen.
Assim seja.

Just a Spirit

The train stopped.
The white-bearded man entered.
Oh no!
Not him again!
My God, does he smell!
It is freezing,
And the man is without footwear
(dirty black, calloused feet)
And without a coat.
One of his eyes glinted.
How can he walk around like that?
He enquired whether I had a cigarette to spare.
I told him I didn't.
Please leave already.

["Stand clear of the closing doors, please."]

Diagonally across from me sits a young man:
Dredlocked, 20-ish.
Homeless?
Not sure.
I did not want to make any assumption.
Digging into his pocket,
He takes out a pack of cigarettes,
Offering one to white-bearded man.
He takes the offered cigarette

And hurriedly exits the train at the next stop.
The young man looks at me,
His eyes soft and kind,
An embarrassing counter to my callousness.
"He's just a spirit having a human experience."
I acknowledged his words of wisdom,
Marveling at his acceptance of the bearded man,
Seeing himself in the man
And the man in himself
His ready acceptance
Putting into bold relief my own disdain.
And then it hit me...
My disdain for the man
Was a disdain of all humanity.

The Universe and Me

"i have taken the nazarite vow...again."
—Sabio

and yes, i accept
i accept (if you say so)
that the status quo is to be how it is
that what happens to us is our paying back
that he is the way he is
because the universe would have it so
that things are the way they are
because the universe would have it so
(an excuse for inactivity...if you ask me)
i accept the power of the universe
to do what it must
and i accept my finiteness
my limitations as a woman
and my inability to change things
i accept the presumptuousness of thinking...
of thinking i can change things
but i also accept my freedom
my freedom to refuse to accept
the unfairness of the status quo
and i accept my freedom to act
to change the status quo
and thus i will act
knowing the futility of my actions

but it is in acting that i affirm my freedom to be
in acting i authenticate my own existence
fully knowing that in such authentication
i might still lose
and by the way...
lest you think otherwise
i accept **Him** too

The Freedom to Care (Or Not)

Every step we take towards humanity,
However small that step,
Is a step in the right direction.
Every attempt to mobilize others
To take that step,
Every smile offered,
Every encouraging word,
Every caring touch—
A hand on the shoulder,
A handshake--
Every act of kindness...
It is a step in the right direction.

If the freedom of the street dweller is assumed--
The freedom to make choices,
To accept the consequences,
Then that pre-supposes my freedom also—
My freedom to show compassion to her (or not),
To feel sorrow for her (or not),
To extend a helping hand to her (or not),
To "save" her however illusory (or not),
Just as she is free
To choose to accept
Or to choose to reject my gestures.
If you're free to judge the street dweller's merits,
Or to speculate about his circumstances,

Or his motives,
Or to form conclusions (without evidence)
As to his character or disposition—
That he is lazy—
Or to put forward the *exceptio probat regulam,*
Or to hold that tough love
Should be the requisite response,
Allow me the freedom also
To defer analysis,
To assume his good intentions,
To assume his weakness
In the face of his overwhelming circumstances,
To figure that it is not simply a matter
Of his needing to man-the-fuck-up
And suddenly receiving clarity of mind
From some tough love approach.
Allow me the freedom to care (or not).

Those Without Sin

Mike and Gwen were excommunicated today.
Well...not excommunicated-excommunicated,
But forbidden to partake in the Lord's Supper.
She was pregnant with his child--
Out of wedlock.
[Whisper] For Nee Kay Shun...
There was actually a ceremony for this...
This excommunion-cation...
This "casting of stones,"
For that is exactly what we did...
We cast stones at the young couple.
Yes, we did.
We...the ones who were without sin.
And I, Andreas Pistis, being the senior Elder—
Though only twenty—
I was required to officiate it.
Then not long after,
We (the ones who were without sin)
We heard the news:
"Michael is dead.
He took his own life." (A nice way of saying...
He committed suicide.)
Was it the sham(e) of excommunion-cation?
Or did we kill him?

"It is better..."

When he was nineteen he heard Fred talk
About his dream of going to the Jamboree.
A former boy scout himself,
He understood the boy's dream.
And to fulfill his dream
He gave him his entire month's paycheck--
A paycheck surely needed that month
To pay the rent, to buy food, to pay the bills.
But he was unshakable in his faith
That **JHWH YRH** would provide
For him and for the four

Fifty years later he saw a young man dying
And sought to give him a chance at living.
He saw him giving up,
And he encouraged him to not give up.
He saw him abandoning hope,
And he offered him a reason to hope.

"I was simply being human,"
He said, "Just being human."
"In the little time I have been given,
All I want to do is use the little **Jah** gave me
To do what little I can
To help those who have little."

The Miracle on Five Plates

We carried ourselves proudly.
None knew the privation we endured-
The pangs of hunger,
The longing for a morsel.
Our source of strength?
Each other and God our Father.
Our source of sustenance?
The nearby cane field.
The bare pantry mocked us.
The empty table taunted us.
Well did we understand Oliver, poor child,
And the widows and the fatherless,
And those overwhelmed by penury,
But we held our heads high,
Daring hunger to do its worse,
Refusing to be humbled,
To be brought down.
We dared to live,
Resisting defeat
While the wolves of starvation
Lay siege around us.
I came home that afternoon,
And what awaited?
A miracle.
A feast.
A feast, the envy of the gods,

A banquet rivaling those of kings.
Five plates,
Five hungry mouths.
The table was set.
No baked meats adorned its surface,
No wine to make glad the heart,
No desserts to transport the soul
To heights of delight,
But a miracle lay in each plate-
Porridge,
The union of grated cassava, sugar, and water,
A feast like none other,
A feast incomparable.

No Meaning in Material Things?!

"Dear Andreas,

Do not worry about my present condition.
I am very happy in my current surroundings.
As for…I make much of whatever I can have…
The material things of this life are fleeting.
They no longer mean much to me.
I prefer the spiritual things of life.
You might believe that I am suffering.
It might also appear to be so to many (smile),
But my present life is a ray of sunshine.
I am very, very happy.
And to a more enlightened atmosphere
I am cheerfully moving on.
So, take care of yourself,
And try to be cheerful and happy at all times.
Be sure also to work hard.
Be diligent in the day-to-day activities of life,
But focus more on the spiritual things of life…

Sincerely,
Your Father"

The Visit

I have about another week to live;
So say my doctors.
I am completely bedridden.
My bones ache constantly,
And my body has grown increasingly weak.
But my spirit remains youthful.
Andreas visited me yesterday.
I had wondered whether he would show up.
He marches to the beat of his own drum.
We have known each other for over a year.
We quickly took to each at our first meeting.
There was something compelling about him--
An innocent passion,
A self-confidence,
A maturity beyond his years,
A seemingly inscrutable depth,
His sharp intellect.
He waved off talks of his intellect,
Claiming it as merely the result of hard work.

We both enjoyed each other's company,
And I knew he liked me a great deal,
Like a little sister of course,
And I adored him as a big brother.
Our favorite spot was the stone bench—
The one under the tree near the main entrance.

Many a wonderful conversation had we there.
The most memorable occurring
The same day I was hospitalized.
He was already there when I showed up...
He sat on the bench,
Unusually quiet,
Brooding.
I pressed him and he opened up,
Talking about the pressure of the expectations.
He hated talks of his genius and brilliance,
Claiming these as nothing more than an illusion.
"I want to study and not be seen.
I want to study in the "dark".
I do not even embrace the ideas I study.
When you think you understand
And that an idea is in your grasp
It soon eludes you,
And the pursuit begins anew.
I am just fascinated by knowledge,
The ephemerality of knowledge that draws me."
We sat there talking until it got dark.
As we parted he giggled boyishly saying,
"I decided to get a C in Philosophy,
And act of freedom on my part.
I am beholden to no-one's expectations."
I laughed, and we went our separate ways.

As I said, he visited me yesterday.
He stood in the doorway of my bedroom,
Not saying a word.
Gradually, he edged closer.
Daveed, who had arrived earlier, greeted him.
He continued to edge closer to the bed.
I was heavily medicated,
But I was very aware and oriented.
I inquired about school,
About some of the professors,
Talked about my transition,
About eagerly anticipating being with the Lord.
He had still not said a word.
I looked at him intently.
I could see the tears welling up in his eyes.
Suddenly, he turned, rushing out of the room.
I knew he was angry,
And I knew at Whom.
That was the last time I saw him.

I grow weaker and weaker...
I still have another two days left.
Will he come?
Will I see him again?

Walking Away

An overcast day...
Dark-grey clouds hovered overhead.
Matching the clouds in the theologian's soul.
(Well...not quite a theologian yet;
He was getting there.)
He sat on a stone bench under a tree,
A focal spot on the verdant property
Housing that place of learning --
For birthing theologians,
Manufacturing "shepherds of sheep,"
Producing winners of souls
(Heralds of the gospel),
Examining God under a microscope,
And cultivating kindness and compassion.

Not far from the place lies a man,
An invisible man,
The sidewalk his habitation.
Day after day those prospective shepherds,
Those soon-to-be theologians and soul-winners,
They would pass him by.
No guidance did they give.
No good news did they share.
No compassion and kindness did they offer.
For those votaries of the Faith
The singular focus was on Ultimate Concern

And on unresolved interpretations and theories.
Submerged in study, they became inured...,
Inured to the man sitting there day after day,
Now merely part of the surrounding landscape,
Enveloped in the smell of excrement and urine,
Displaced, disenfranchised, disgraced,
His face a portrait of suffering...
His body a repository of pain...
Sitting or lying there hungry and thirsty,
Sitting or lying on the sidewalk partially naked,
Matted hair, dark, dry skin,
A dirty burlap covering his loins,
And on his right leg as if offered for scrutiny
A patch of raw, fetid flesh oozing pus,
A banquet for the flies buzzing around.

The picture begging the obvious questions:
"Is man no more than this?"
Or...
Why would God....?

That day under the tree the theologian sat,
A potential winner of souls,
A promising shepherd of sheep,
His soul adrift, his mind embattled.
He found no comfort in Ultimate concern.

No comfort found he in God's transcendence.
God seemed silent, distant.
He was nowhere near or immanent.
"Out of the depths I cry unto You, O Lord."

A loud "Bang!" punctuates the noonday silence,
Freeing him from the onslaught of nothingness.
He walks out of the grounds to investigate,
The only one arriving on the scene
On that quiet street under the unbearable sun.
A vehicle lies twisted against the concrete wall.
Not too far away on the ground...
Matted hair, dark, dry skin,
A burlap sack around his loins.
Raw, fetid flesh exposed on his right leg
(The flies refusing to leave the banquet),
The right leg broken in half...
The lower half lying at a right angle.
Human excrement filled the afternoon air.
A barely audible whimper comes from the man.
"... not with a bang, but with a whimper."

Still the only one on the scene...,
He offers no help.
He speaks not a word,...
He just takes one look.

That future winner of souls,
That potential shepherd of sheep,
The soon-to-be-Theologian.
One look he took,
And he walked away.
He went back to the spot under the tree.
On the stone bench under the tree he sat down
And there wept and wept and wept…
"By the rivers of Babylon… "
In that place, under the tree…
That winner of souls,
That shepherd of sheep,
That soon-to-be-Theologian....
Like Ivan Karamazov,
He "refused the ticket."
He could not in good conscience
Be in Heaven
With Hell next door.

A Little Lamb's Plea

Love sees the sorrowful tears that flow,
Oozing softly before the morning's glow,
When all has succumbed to the quiet deep
And restless awareness, acknowledging defeat,
Becomes the ward of comforting sleep.

Love hears the anguish in the suppliant's wails
And feels the desperation in the biting of nails
While the heart pounds in throbbing fear,
Beating out its desperate message so clear:
"Where, O where are You my Adonai dear?"

Love is His comforting, caring arm
Extending tenderness and comfort warm,
Encircling me and drawing me near,
And with gentle words soothing my fear,
Assuring me He is always there.

Love is that determined, silent prayer
That wafts it way to our Loving Shepherd's ear,
Asking of grace and my soul to keep,
Whilst wandering in Death's valley deep...
Keep Thy little lamb, Lord, in safety keep.

"Then I became an adult –
argumentative, analytical,
apprehensive..."

Unilateral Banter

It happened again last night.
That sultry exchange
Between him and me.
That's the other thing--
Not sure he is a he,
Or a she,
Or an it,
But that's for further deliberation.
The exchange was heated.
Call it a conversation
If you will,
But as conversations go
It was all over the place -
More like a hemorrhaging to me.
I believe I nodded off at one point.
Bored maybe?
Or just plain tired.

After all,
It was just another busy day,
Even had a fight with
You-Know-Who,
But damn, I needed that.
Conflict is cathartic.
Like a transfusion?

But then again
I should know;
I belong to the 'weaker sex.'
"I don't believe he
Heard a word I said."
Must be tough having to listen daily
To so many.
All unilateral banter anyway.
Mere transpositions
Of wishes and desires.
And heaven knows
We humans desire much ---
Now there goes
My Garden of Spice opportunity.
So, why am I here again?
Feeling loved and unloved,
Surrounded by everyone
But lonely still?

Like getting heckled while performing,
A blueprint for nihilism, really,
But I tore that up long ago,
Having experienced first-hand
Subjugation by Truth.
What did you say
Your name was again?

I guess I missed the point.
No one asked my opinion.
Don't I get to have a say?
But I ramble on.
What I really intended
Was an outpouring,
You know…
Like getting things
Off the chest.
But I do give a shit…
Ah…life's fluctuations,
Its ebb and flow
Purposeful today,
But tomorrow?
Futile and meaningless.
Yesterday?
Forgotten.
So...about that conversation,

Or should I say, 'exchange.'
Nothing came of it.
What else is new?
We shall try again tomorrow,
Or at least,
I shall try again tomorrow
Since I doubt that He really gives a shit.

My Name is Uzit

*I*gnored are the anguish
And the pain I endure;
Disregarded is the suffering
Ruthlessly brought upon me
To showcase righteousness,
To demonstrate a point.
Alas the boastful claim...
"Have you taken notice of...?"
Like a breeder displaying
His prized thoroughbred,
Or like an infant showing off
Its recently acquired toy.
No consideration given to my loss,
But to the hounds of grief thrown.
One moment they were there,
And then suddenly no more.
All destroyed, pitilessly wiped out,
Slaughtered like helpless lambs.
Not one, not two, not three,
But all ten – gone in an instant,
Rudely torn from this sacred earth,
Three girls, seven boys, together,
Whom these languid breasts gave suck,
Beloved fruits of my womb,
Brought forth in extreme pain
And all the more loved and treasured.

The river of my tears has dried up,
Blood now flows from my eyes,
Springing up from a hollow heart
Weighed down and by sorrow burdened,
My life now a useless void,
Adrift in a maze of grey,
All hope utterly destroyed,
Every reason to be, inconsequential,
And motherhood made insignificant.
And yet, in all my grief and pain,
Staying faithful and true to him
To whom for better or for worse
I pledged to stay -
Day and night attending to him
While silently enduring his sickness,
His vile sores, his foul breath,
And the stench of his excrement.
O the horror! O the agony!
Deceased children, diseased spouse.
O the agony! O the horror!
A wife's service undisclosed,
A mother's pain overlooked,
A mother eternally vilified
For offering the loving admonition,
"Curse God, and die."

A Wager

And the question, "Have you considered...?"
And then the consideration,
And then the game...the game began.
The dice were rolled, six all told.
He had called odd,
And I became his to prod
Like a pliant and docile cow.
With "*heroic carelessness and lightheartedness*"
He gambled on my soul and won.
But there was no need, no need at all.
I would willingly have gone.
Willingly would I have given my soul
For the Confliction,
For the Contrary,
For the Contradiction,
To the Fire, to Agni,
To Him,
For the Life not worth living.
I had had enough of the other One,
The old One with the perpetual frown,
Dressed always in inaccessible white,
He who had made me his footstool
Upon which to rest His feet,
His lame, yellow-white, varicosed feet.
It was his idea, this game of dice,
Perhaps in a puerile moment of caprice,

Losing me without regard for the price.
Fire, Fire, Burn!
Burn, Burn, Burn!
Play the harmonica while Heaven burns.

This sulfurous descent is stifling.
He assumed my moral excellence.
I cannot breathe...
I was not what he thought I was.
I cannot breathe...
He took the risk, and sealed my fate,
I cannot breathe...
Pinning his hope on my uprightness.
Air, Air is what I need.
So down we plunge, engulfed
In an oppressive and palpable suffocation,
Engulfed in the darkness...the thick darkness,
The horror of a thick darkness.
Something good will come of this, I am certain.
Can we pretend we are lovers?
You won me, but I chose You first,
My Dark falling Star,
Falling...
Falling into a doomed and happy oblivion.
Can we kiss this nightmare away?
Tell me something good will come of this.

From Faith to Faith

Fire, Fire, Burn!

Bless me, Father, for I have...
In this dark and cramped enclosure.
Alas! I still thirst.
The Water from the stoup of stone
Quenched me not.
I poured the Water over my head,
And still I am not pure,
Still I am not cleansed...
For I have sinned.
I cannot recall the last time...
The fault is mine; the choice was mine.
He won me, but I chose Him first,
My Dark fallen Star of the morning.
That Law, Father,...that tablet of stone,
Does it say anything about a daughter's wife?
She is not my neighbor;
I am her mother - I gave her life.
She is my offspring.
I coveted my daughter's wife.
The Water covers my head.
I cannot breathe,
I cannot breathe...
Air, not penance,
Air is what I need.

Burn, Burn, Burn!

You came to me in a dream,
And I reached out to touch you,
Hoping you'd stroke my hair once again,
But you retreated into the darkness.
Then there you were again
Dancing with dogs and with that He-goat,
My Lightening falling from Heaven,
Cut down by you to the ground.
I reached out to touch you,
Hoping you would call my name, as before,
And again you retreated into the thick darkness,
Leaving resentment in your wake.
I had let you down, for I chose Him.
And my Bhumi, my Earth, opened up--
For it was time, the time of harvest.
My Mother, my Earth,
She opened her arms to embrace me,
As if to say, "All is well."
As if to say, "You are safe;
All is well."
And indeed something good will come of this,
Will it not?
For goodness is in plentiful supply,
And wickedness is scarce and in demand

From Faith to Faith

And appears the more valuable.
But it is time, and everything must return.
Ashes to Dust, and Dust to Earth.
It is time;
The time has come,
But everything will be born again.
Is it not so?
Promise me...
Promise me
That everything will be born again.
Play the harmonica while Heaven burns.

The Unprepared

Those vacuous and haunting stares
Of hollow and illusory expectations,
Painted on weary and vacant faces,
Vapid mirrors of my own emptiness.
De-brained and with excised hearts,
We sit shoulder to shoulder,
On the same fruitless journey.
Of similar composition,
And of the same sanguine flow
Now dried up for want of passion.

Unmindful of one another,
We are lost - not in thought - just lost,
Estranged from ourselves
And from each other alienated,
Caught up in a world of Ones,
Seemingly engaged but disengaged;
Ensnared in a world of Zeroes.
We are wooed by posters and signs,
Hypnotized by images and texts.
Everything around us speaks.

Meanwhile we remain inert and mute,
Exuding apathy and indifference,
Going and returning,
Going and returning,

From Faith to Faith

Caught between two parentheses
Of inane terminal points.
And despite all our practice for life,
Still without knowledge of how to live.
And lacking the knowledge of how to live,
Ill-prepared to die.

Falling Lightening

My name is Lucifer.
You look repulsed,
Somewhat apprehensive,
And a bit uncomfortable -
Just an observation.
It means "bringing light" -
My name, that is,
But that's as far as it goes -
The meaning has no relation
To who I am in essence.

A professor of philosophy and literature
(The works of dead white men),
I was twice married,
With four children the result.
I am a rebel who follows the rules,
But every once in a while
I do cross the line or make mistakes,
Some more egregious than others.
Yes, I do love my name;

The other Lucifer?
I think he got a bum rap.
He was only speaking his mind,
Got pissed off at the system,
Calling tyranny as he saw it.

His revolution was brutally crushed.
I believe Michael set him up...

Looks like you are pissed
At what I have said.
But never mind me;
My imagination often takes flight.
My mother (God rest her dear soul)
Always said I had a wild imagination.
My name is Lucifer;
It means "bringing light",
But that's as far as it goes for me -
The meaning has no relation
To who I am in essence.
Still...what cruelty to name a child such,
Lucifer.
Imagine the stigma,
The burden I must carry,
But I am not my name.

A Pact

Just when I thought the deal sealed
You propose a renegotiation.
I should have anticipated this,
Knowing your reputation for deception
And knowing of your kinship to...
To...Mephistophles
And of your collusion
In Gretchen's seduction
To satisfy the lust
Of that disgruntled scholar
In quest of unlimited knowledge
And, I might add, pleasures,
Easily acquired these days at one's leisure
From that thing called the Web.
And if I might ask by the way,
What is his status these days?
Mephistophles I mean, not the scholar –
Since both your art is no longer in demand,
Superannuated because of the digital eon.
What is his status these days?
He can no longer walk, you say?
Lame in both feet?
No roaming back and forth?
A reprieve then.

Imagine the world without his deceit.

From Faith to Faith

I had my dealings with him in the past;
It has certainly been a while.
I know first-hand his devious guile.
You see that man sitting across from us?
The one unabashedly picking his nose?
Gross, isn't it?
Why do they all do that?
Must be an ethnic thing I suppose.
But back to your proposition...
You are in no position to make demands
Considering the old times are past gone
When you two had the upper hand –
You and Mephisto I mean.
Your influence is still regarded by some,
But the world you once dominated...
It has moved on.
Your help is far less needed these days
Since barely any effort is required
To effect a malevolent outcome.
And of course you are not feared anymore
As you were both feared in times before.
We humans, at our worst,
Are more to be feared than you two.

And how has the once powerful and feared
Become the stuff of old wives' tale?

But I could certainly make use of you still,
Of course, on my terms
And according to my will.
Should I offer that pregnant lady my seat?
I don't usually offer women my seat;
You now why?
For fear they will refuse my good deed,
Or my attempt at a good deed.
Plus, I'm too often busy writing to care...
Writing poetry.
The rhythm of existence?
That's what you call poetry?
I call it a duplicitous distortion of reality,
Presented as reflection on the sublime
But in reality a reflection on nothing –
Nonsense that sounds pleasing to the ear,
Merely underlying the poet's insignificance.
The Sophist, if indeed he was such,
In his "Ion" said as much.
This is your stop.
Here...
Do not forget this.
Do not leave without your walking stick.
You said you have an appointment?
With someone about to die
Or with someone recently dead?

From Faith to Faith

I find that rather inane.
How about a memorial for the living...
A memorial for the living instead?
My regards to old Mephisto, Mephistoples…
And be careful up there.
It's 3:00 A.M. -
The hour of humans.
Beware.

The Question

And shall I then dare ask the burning question,
For so long frozen within my restless soul,
Imbuing my tongue with aching numbness,
And igniting that rabid percussion in my chest?

And must I lose this transient and uneasy peace
When bloodstains adorn pages dull and musty,
Or memory's pain escapes its weighty chains
Like shadows ruthlessly torn from the dead?

And shall I then proceed with the transaction,
Accept the inevitable, or negotiate a deferment,
Knowing that choice, in reality, does not exist,
But that it is just the elusive dream of fools?

And must I, obsequiously, embrace your terms
And in dejection walk away wringing my hands
Like a dog chased off, its tail between its legs
And complaining about the unfairness of it all?

And can I will that this be but a withered dream
Trapped in a bush like the sacrificial substitute?
A fading dream in which life begins to die soon after birth
And begins to live as soon as it dies?

So, do I dare ask the question,

From Faith to Faith

Risking exposure of my soul, my vulnerabilities,
The eternal summons, the dark confrontation?
Will He dare answer or be open to compromise?

The Last Call

Sitting there, simply sitting there,
Staring blankly at the dubious lights
And thinking effortlessly about
That recalcitrant hole in my pocketbook,
There like an incessant aching tooth
And incongruous with the elegance
That is my sensuous exterior, or…that 'was'...
I am nonplussed and filled
With a singular, heavy incredulity
At the stark reality
Of my insignificance,
That I, at some juncture,
Might lose the companionship -
Woe is me! - of consciousness.
But I protest, refusing to accept
Non-being as an option.
Rather would I embrace awareness
In that place "where the worm
Dies not and the fire is not quenched"
Than be bereft of soul and spirit.
I desire life - in any form, in any place.
Is it too much to ask?
To desire to exist on my terms?

"Do you have a light?"

From Faith to Faith

I feel like that cleaning rag -
The cloth you are using to wipe the countertop -
Cold, worn-out, wrinkled, dispensable.
A black eye hidden behind sunglasses,
And the three-day old makeup forming
A doomed alliance with tears and sweat.
Existenz (with a zee)? Essence? Whatever!
It is fitting, then, the annoyance I feel
On account of my unshaved legs,
Broken nails, missing front tooth,
Knocked out a long, long time ago
(But that's another story);
I don't smile anymore these days,
Busy drowning my sorrows and guilt in 'piss'.
Now if i could only find my lipstick...

Yes. I would like another one, please.

I lost two of them within a year.
I won't talk about the pain;
The pain is one thing, the guilt is another.
I'd rather the former than the latter.
No, I am not talking about the tooth;
That occurred a really long time ago.
He does not fight fairly at all, you know;
One would expect better of Him.

We wrestled all night - until daybreak;
Yes, He and I.
Who did you think?
Surprisingly, I was holding my own.
Stubborn, like my mother, I yielded not.
I said to Him, "I will not let You go..."
Then, suddenly, an explosion of pain,
And the expelling of blood and a tooth,
Ha Ha! My Blessing, I suppose.

Could you pass me the ashtray, please?

Yes, the guilt…, it sticks to you
Like the foulness of decaying flesh,
Like a mouth of bad breath,
Like anal leachate.
That the oldest remains is no consolation,
No one should ever be in my situation.
In the space of one year! Imagine that!
Awakened to death!
Oh, the guilt, the guilt!
Not the horror, but the guilt!
For Kurtz it was the horror, for me, the guilt.
It's my fault; I didn't do enough...
In the space of one year! Oh God!
Me? No, I don't blame Him.

From Faith to Faith

He will do and must do that which He must,
I would rather me than Him.
I hold Him no ill-will or malice,
In fact, I feel sad for Him.

I think that man over there is checking me out.

No parent should have to bury her child.
I remember a conversation with my youngest,
"How did I get the scars on my leg...?
You remember how I said
That when I am anxious I self-mutilate?
Well...that's what happened.
What made me anxious? Church.
How did Church make me anxious?
Well, I heard this sermon...
Yes, it was about hell."
Then, with tears streaming down my face,
I said to her,...My dearest,
If He sends you to that place,
I will find you in that place, wherever you are,
Whether in Hell or someplace worse.
I will give back my ticket to go be with you

Where is the rest room?

So here I sit, against the backdrop
Of clinking glasses and amidst the din
Of distorted and meaningless conversations.
Rob Thomas and Santana vie for attention,
But I have not gotten to my point.
I evade it like the matador avoids his bull,
As I, for years, always avoided going home,
Because my greatest fear awaits.
No, not the guilt, not the guilt at all,
But my imagination, my creation;
It has plagued me since a child,
And given life by a lonely child's imagination,
A hell than which no greater can be conceived...

"Excuse me, Miss; that's the signal for Last Call."

[*Dard bhee tu, Chain bhee tu....*]
A quick swipe at the lonely, sorrowful tear
That managed to escape past old mascara,
One last drag on a doleful looking cigarette,
And I reluctantly stumbled out into the night…
[*Aawaaz maein naa duunga…*]

Of Broken Dreams

I am witness to the cold, stone statue
Shedding a miraculous tear
On behalf of an estranged world,
Amidst sacred voices that speak not,
And where fear breathes its last
To the melancholy beat of nothingness.
The people made the choice, I say,
Of death and of life, drawing lots,
Unmindful of the complaints of the dead.
The expectation of a bitter kiss
And at some point thirty pieces returned,
That's all that can be hoped for.
Or would you rather the stench
Of those numbered among the living?
I am no Iscariot; I resent the comparison,
But I would happily point Him out, with a kiss.
I would, but without the mawkish guilt.
So here we are planting dainty illusions
And reaping mildewed despair,
Sowing calculated and thought-out hope
And harvesting withered promises
In a parched, unyielding, and bitter land
Where the cries of the oppressed are eviscerated
And justice is merely an inconvenience.

And so continues the unabated boredom,

Without compensation for carrying crosses.
You misunderstand me, as usual.
I am no prophet of doom;
I find that too fashionable for my taste.
I shed the Lamb's clothing ages ago.
Or was it Sheep's clothing? Perfidious.
They are still there in my pocket,
Those dismantled dreams undreamt,
The broken remains of hope long lost
And trapped beneath a sordid gravestone
From which not even a tear can flow.
I struck it twice with a rod, and nothing.
And yet, we persevere, clinging, holding on,
Etherized by a moment's ephemeral pleasure
Only to be reawakened again too soon to life.
Shall we raise misguided prayers from ashes?
Shall we build tombs from ruined churches?
O lasting and abiding city, we seek you;
There, in the cold earth beneath, we seek you,
Where none discriminates, where exists
Neither young or old, rich or poor,
Uncomely or beautiful, ignorant or wise,
The hopeful or the hopeless,
The good or the evil,
But only the hapless race of humanity
Who, for all its faults, desires to be loved still.

From Faith to Faith

And so, O Son of Humankind,
Be kind to the dead.
Awake us not but let us sleep.
We beseech You.
Let us sleep.

Indictment

Picture the scene
A dark alleyway intersecting a quiet street
The street is littered with refuse
On the sidewalk a garbage bin
A “vagrant” hovers over it
Burlap fabric covering his nakedness
[He looks familiar doesn’t he?]

A musician walks by, sees the vagrant
He stops, looks at the impoverished
And continues walking…
A book comes flying from the alleyway
Hits the artist on his head
He scurries off...surprised, afraid

A politician walks by
He too stops and looks at the captive
He continues walking…
The books also strikes him on the head
As if out of nowhere, from the alleyway
He too scurries off surprised and afraid
The vagrant is still hovering over the trash bin
Oblivious to the goings on around him

A preacher walks by,
A Bible dotingly cradled in his right forearm

He stops and looks at the "blind" vagrant
He continues walking...
The Word comes flying from the alleyway
Hits him on the side of his head
Surprised and afraid, he scurries off

Still oblivious, the vagrant ends his search
He recovers no food scrap
The garbage bin yields no good news
Offers no release from captive hunger
He stands scratching his dredlocked head
Then from the alleyway the book comes flying
Striking him on the head and landing at his feet
He looks down at the book
A black hardcover book
"Holy Bible" on the front cover
Not afraid, just surprised,
He picks up the book
And angrily hurls it back into the alleyway
Suddenly, from the alleyway
Interrupting the silence...
a loud "Ouch!"
The oppressed sucks his teeth, turns
And continues down the lonely street
His sole objective - finding a garbage bin.

Whose Side Are You On?

We've had my suspicions about You.
More and more they're being confirmed.
All the lofty and misleading homilies,
All this talk about You,
About You being on the side of the oppressed,
We are finding hard to believe these days.
The colorless, light-skinned ones
Seem to find more favor with You.
You make them victorious in all the wars,
Have given them greater economic advantage,
And allow them to win in everything.
What's the use of clasped hands,
Or the benefits of closed eyes,
Or the utility of calloused knees?
We have seen where those have gotten many.
In the final analysis the suppliants' upraised arms
Availeth nothing –
So it seems.
It appears that You do not like us -
The people of color,
The darker skinned,
The poorer nations…
You give us very little to cheer about.
In vain we wait for a break-through.
The result of our hopes is always the same -
Dashed to pieces,

From Faith to Faith

Foundered on the rock of misplaced hope.
“Shall we look up to the hills?
From whence does our help come?”

I know the answer I should give,
But I lack the confidence to say it.

Of Shadow and Substance

A quiet walk in a painted landscape
On a bright and sunny summer's day
Offers the golden sun without its warmth
As colorful flowers in bedazzling array
Their mellifluous fragrance withhold.
Even the feathered musicians balk,
Muted, as if inoculated from persuasion,
Their songs forever imprisoned in a moment
While Time, in ponderous contemplation,
Seems lost, as if in quest for some purpose,
Dazed, dreamlike, and sullenly transfixed,
Having the appearance of form and life
But eerily soulless and void of texture.
Alone and without You
I wander along that now worn-out path
Winding its way like a fast-fading dream
Through hurried brushstrokes of vibrant green,
Among inertly torpid trees and stagnant leaves
Drowned in a vapid, haunting silence.
But from this vivid eruption of sterile beauty,
Incandescent, cacophonic, verdant, prismatic,
Life, as if mortified, long made its hasty retreat,
Leaving behind a morbid contradiction,
The apparent and the essential in opposition,
A bland canvas of shadows without substance,

And I, lonely itinerant, now weary and lost,
Doomed to traverse this vista of indifference.
And where are You when I most need You?

Samsara

And so I arrived, amidst pain and joy
But with no recollection of the event
Nor any clear idea as to my purpose.
And then began my ruthless education
The ordeal of living and learning.
To what end?
I cannot tell.
But this much I know,
That in time, I must of necessity depart.
And perhaps I shall return again,
But I wonder at the point of it all.

"...No God"

And sitting on Your Olympus of morality,
All those long years You judged me,
Receiving praise untold for uprightness
While the other stood exposed, condemned,
Often censored and brutally punished,
Her body the terminal of Your blows.
Mine own eyes did observe her crime,
And my finger against her bore witness,
While of Your fidelity my mouth testified
And continuing thus unto this day
Supporting the lie of Your untaintedness -
A lie indeed hidden all these years,
But now by a single revelation revealed.
And all these years, all these long years,
Under Your false standard I lived,
Enduring Your constant chastisements,
Holding You impeccable and blameless,
Praising to all and sundry Your uprightness
While living with your last words to me,
Those words that bore witness against me
Of my failure to measure up to You,
To Your standard which now barely stands.
Words, that I concluded marked my own doom,
The utterance of a dying Father's curse.
But with this revelation, from that curse I'm free,
For in truth now I find that You are no God,

All along a mindless and empty declaration.
And since by far I stand more upright than You,
Tell me, who gave You the right
To be "disappointed in" me?

Of the Human Heart

Deceitful and desperately wicked?
To such stern characterization
Allow me (acknowledging your omnipotence),
With fear and trembling to object.
I will find ten righteous, yea, twenty.
I will for scrutiny hold up the heart,
That inviolable symbol of Humanity.
I offer Thelma and Miriam, saintly women
Such as the world has never seen -
Other than the venerable Agnes Gonxha,
Mother to countless multitudes,
Or the bespectacled Bapu, Mohandas,
Who, as the bearded Nazarene commanded us,
Turned the other cheek, eschewing violence,
Or Father Oscar Romero who lost his life
Speaking out on behalf of the oppressed,
Or the many who with each passing day
Offer a kind word here or a few mites there,
Giving of themselves, unrewarded, unsung,
Or a father sacrificing all for his family,
Or a mother moving heaven and earth
To provide her children life's necessities.
Far and near, in every corner of the earth,
In big cities, in hamlets, in towns, in villages,
Among Arabs, among Jews,
Among Blacks, among Whites,

Among Asians, among Indigenes,
Among the indigent and among the affluent,
Among homosexuals, among heterosexuals,
Among all religions and nationalities,
Compassion, benevolence, magnanimity, mercy,
Humanity's sacred and inestimable gifts to itself
Transcending race, creed, and status,
Providing hope in the face of hopelessness
And love where none seems to exist.
And so, with utmost pride,
I, this ordinary woman, numbers myself,
Esteem myself fortunate to be,
Among those who are called Humans.

Coming and Going

And just as I am getting used to the place
I find out that I must leave,
But from whence I came I cannot say,
Nor of my destination
Give an accurate account,
Nor of my purpose here.
Fuzzy indeed is my beginning,
Behind which is an impenetrable blackness.
Throughout my stay I had hoped for clarity
As to my end or my *raison d'être*,
But nothing was forthcoming.
With my accomplishments here I am satisfied
And did receive just due for good and ill,
Though some have carried on
About future emoluments beyond this place,
Either advantageous or otherwise.
Others talk of my having been here before
(Of that I have no recollection)
And that this time around
I am merely making reparations.
For what? I know not.
Strange indeed that of all these things
Everyone else seems to know but I.
With conviction and certainty do they speak,
But as to the eventual interment or cremation,
As to my evaporation into nothingness,

All I can say is,
What a waste!

Debris

[I]

Sorry, I have no idea what day it is today;
It could be Sunday or Wednesday or Friday.
All I know is that it is freezing cold outside.
But as I was saying to you before the question,
I voted for neither candidate last November.
Of course I was given the usual admonition,
The one that seems to criminalize non-voting,
Including the necessity of choosing the less evil.
But I reject the lesser-of-two-evils principle.
Evil is evil.
It cannot be quantified.
It cannot be qualitatively differentiated.
By choosing none, I am negating evil altogether.
Is the individual who slaughters one person
Less evil than the one who slaughters two?
Or is the church-going dictator less evil
Than the dictator who is an avowed atheist?
Anyone supporting the lesser evil principle
Must consider the inviolable right of the Moon
In sustaining the universal appeal of dignity.
For how can a pro-creative imagination
Withstand the assault of reason on cellphones,
Or how can that luminary be adumbrated?
The answer is in the question, your honor.
Or blowing somewhere in the northeast wind.

Like socialists coming together with capitalists,
Both vigorously seeking to overthrow fascism.

[II]
You have that puzzled look on your face.
You wonder at the strange faces I make.
That is to scare them away, the little rascals.
They follow me everywhere I go, annoying me,
Interrupting my conversation, poking me.
I found an effective way to ward them off -
Making scary faces, baring my teeth.
Of course you don't see them now;
I just scared them off, but they will be back.
Ladies and gentlemen, thank you very much,
Thank you for allowing me to express...
To express my anger and my disapproval.
For every action there is an opposite and...
There is an opposite and equal reaction.
You want to know what they look like?
Didn't you see them crawling around,
Diaper-clad two-year olds on hands and knees?
There's one! Fricking little rascal!
See how quickly he scurried away?
I tell ya, the scary face works every time.

[III]
Lean over here…
My boyfriend and I…
Well, we are not having sex anymore.
He says that I smell,
That I have bad breath.
He also thinks my beard is too long,
But I like the Che Guevara look..
We got into a heated argument the other day.
I ended up punching the mirror in anger,
Hence the swollen and scarred knuckles.
It's not my fault really.
It's the bathroom.
There are hidden cameras in the bathroom.
They are watching me closely, you know,
Watching and noting my every move.
In the toothpaste there is a particular chemical
Put there specially to get into my thoughts,
But I am on to them.
I am ahead of them.
Take a look at this –
Aluminum foil.
Ingenious eh?
Put in my cap so they can't penetrate my head.
The foil breaks up the electronic signals.

[IV]
Sad isn't it, the deaths of those teens in Brasil.
Could you imagine the grief of their parents?
A child should not die before a mother or father.
Such a thing goes counter to universal law…
There are those voices again; you hear them?
They are always talking about me.
Do you hear them?
Sometimes they tell me to do things...
Anyway…
But such events raise all kinds of questions,
Especially questions of ultimate concern –
Our place in the universe, good and evil,
The relationship of God (assuming He exists),
To the rest of us
And in the larger scheme of things.
You see that car parked outside the restaurant?
Don't look!
It is a grey SUV with tinted windows.
They are in there with their electronic gadgets,
Trying to withdraw my thoughts from my brain.
But I have the tin foil in my cap, remember?
Soon they will get frustrated and take off.
Sometimes they send winged horses to...
Ladies and gentlemen, thank you very much,
Thank you for allowing me to express…

To express my anger and my disapproval.
Oh...I forgot...
I had a nightmare last night,
And I cried out for my mommy.

[V]
The earth orbits,
Moving ever nearer, ever nearer,
Pulled in closer and closer to the Golden Orb.
I see my image in the windowpane.
I seek myself, but He flees, escaping me,
And my own self I cannot win.
And so, alas, my friend,
To have what we would have,
(And I desire not much)
To have what we would have,
We speak not what we mean.

Conversation with Yama

You are no more than a bridge
Between here and there.
Your air of self-importance I resent.
My name? I assumed you knew.
Andreas...Andreas Pistis.
Why do you laugh?
Did I say something funny?
Anyway...getting back to what I was saying...
Your unannounced visitations,
Your tendency to just show up,
I find highly unacceptable.
I frankly do not mind you showing up,
But the courtesy of a heads-up
Would be greatly appreciated.
You know, like a two-week's notice,
Or even two months,
So we can get our shit together –
Tie up loose ends,
Right wrongs,
Make amends,
Do something good,
Have a last blast,
Say our goodbyes,
Fulfill broken promises,
Find forgiveness –
With perhaps a severance payment,

Instead of just arbitrary termination.
But what do you care?
You are only doing your job.
I don't blame you for doing your job
Well, not your job, but His job,
The Big Cheese, His job.
A better system is what we need.
Would I accept immortality or longevity?
Forget longevity and immortality.
Those would be worse by far.
I guess it's the status quo then,
But I still think a better system is needed.
Me? Afraid of you?
No, not in the least.
On the contrary, I find you over-rated,
Ridiculous, laughable, an annoyance really,
And on occasions, fascinating.
Most people fear you.
I do not; not anymore anyway.
I used to when I was a child
And also as a teen and young adult,
"But now that I am a man,
I have put away such...(fears)."
Our departure is inevitable
I do understand and accept that,
But I find it pointless, a waste.

I told you already; don't you get it?
I have no fear of you,
Not afraid to meet you face to face,
Not afraid to look you in the eyes,
For, to fear you is to fear life,
And I am not afraid to live.

Have You Heard?

And why do I marvel
That as the shadows flee
The oak leaf fades
Then falls to ground
And am uneasy
That it is so soon
Nothing but dust?

And why do some use
Its sudden passing
As sermonic homily
About our future habitation
Either in some sultry place
Or in some dreary land
Of milk and honey?

And do you hear the sages
Warning of life's brevity
The need to live well
Suddenly philosophical
In the face of the inscrutable
Taking life seriously
Until soon forgotten in living?

And will we not marvel again
When another leaf fades

And then falls to the ground,
Becoming uneasy
That it is so soon but dust
And forgetting that such is our path
In the cycle of birth, living, and dying?

Path to Perdition

The road ahead is the one she'll choose,
Paying no mind to the objections of her muse.
It seemed the right choice for her to make
Since it's the way few appear to take.
Except for some box-thorn along her path,
She anticipated no overwhelming aftermath.
But wait!
Didn't some wise person something once say
About snares and thorns along the way,
That such is found where the froward walk?
But this traveler is deterred by no Jagannath.
She could care less about the impending wrath.
Her path she must follow.
That well she knows.
And consumed by yearning,
She's constrained to go.

Fire in 'Haza

And up high the CBUs are primed.
The little tinder laughs and plays below.
His weary kindling housecleans and cooks.
At work gardening outside is his father—
Fuel for the fire soon to rain down on the family,
Mere expendables.

Burn, Strip-full of vile sub-humans.
Burn, City of cockroaches.
Impassion the vengeful.
Ignite their hate.
Inflate their illusion of being the chosen of God
Fulfill their invention of land divinely promised.

Too Soon the Flowers Bloom

Do you remember that sweltering day
When at Rockstone's Junction we arrived,
Our aching feet screaming for repose,
And our relief and the indescribable joy
At our brief reprieve from the noonday sun?

How can I ever forget —
Haunted still by that day's memory,
Burdened and bound by shame,
Weighed down by guilt
And by feelings of complicity consumed?

Indeed its effect on you I do recollect.
That day welcomed by our wizened host,
Up in years as his grey locks showed,
Freely sharing his tiny shack with us
And availing us of rations and respite.

Then that old Morris Oxford pulled up,
Bringing to a brief pause talk of my trek -
My quixotic adventure through the forest,
You, my SanchoPanza, and I pursuing the wind,
Fighting windmills.

A Morris Oxford was it?
I hardly noticed, as firmly fixed were my eyes

On the child that alighted from that old relic.
A child--barely thirteen--
Carrying in her arms a child, recently born.

Rescued from a life of hardship and poverty -
That was the story told to us by our aged host.
An arrangement made with the girl's mother -
Herself single, with six hungry children to feed,
Plus her thirteen-year-old, herself now a mother.

And I remember your words
When of the girl's situation he spoke.
You said,
"Ah..., what a horrifying anomaly it is
When too soon, all too soon, the flower blooms."

Shaded from the oppressive sun,
We reclined in hammocks that day,
Engaging our host in mirthful banter,
Our thirsts quenched by cold beer,
And sated from a meal of fresh fish.

O, too quickly the hours flew by.
Then between beer and banter
Of the "arrangement" we learned more -
Far from being paternal or altruistic,

Its singular intent?...the comfort of our host.

Too well I remember our exchange of glances,
Your incredulity at the realization,
Your desire to quickly retreat from that place,
Your silence as we continued along the trail
And how in that moment God felt distant,
The silence screaming His absence.

That Which is Needed

How about...
A simple stand-in for that which is?
And not for the want of presence,
Or for lack of function,
Or for a paucity of motivation,
But just to reinforce the essence.

Let's say...
A temporary distraction of sorts,
Something to sate the inclination,
An agreed upon arrangement,
Nothing more than a transaction.

The upside...?
Bringing rainshine and sunfall,
A guarantee of staying in place
And the affirmation of permanence.
A win-win situation without a doubt
Don't you think...?

Oh...And one other thing...
There are no preferences.
Nothing is impermissible.

The Messenger

And that saintly man
As on his bed of death did lay
Breathing his last precious breath
Took the hand of her who sat beside him.
They were linked in the sacred silence.
And so they sat in that silence sweet
Until broken by her question.
"You remember when I first saw you
How I asked whether you were an angel,
And you gave me that incredulous look?
That was my thought then,
That you looked like an angel,
And you do look like an angel now."
And with a gentle squeeze and a weak smile
That venerable man gave answer,
"Woman, I wronged you once,
And for that I do ask your forgiveness,
But for my many infidelities
Your forgiveness I do not seek,
For, to falling in love,
I have always been vulnerable."
To which she replied,
"I know, my love; I know."
And with one last breath
He departed this life he loved so well.

Living in This World

I don't know how to live
in a world without compassion.
I don't know how to live
in a world that values principles over persons.
I don't know how to live
in a world that prefers diatribe over dialogue.
I don't know how to live
in this world.

Choice and Preference

Like I said to the one named Faith,
My preference is to live the simple life
With the wife of my youth,
Holding the hands of my children
And, following the old gardener's advice
To the consummate optimist, Candide,
Simply tend my own garden.
I told her I preferred a life without knowing,
A life unencumbered by source theories—
Julius Welhausen's Documentary Hypothesis,
Or whether there were two Isaiahs,
Whether the Sacred text is the Word of God
Or whether it merely contains the Word of God,
The primacy of reason over faith or vice versa,
Regarding the Gospel – kerygma or myth,
The Christ of faith or the Jesus of history,
God's transcendence vs His immanence,
And all the theological debates *ad infinitum.*
I told her that it matters not to me
Whether God were one or three,
Whether He (She or It) were good or evil.
"Just give me a life of toil over study," I said,
"I would readily stay far away from 'The Tree'",
But I know myself.
I would always harbor a desire for its Fruit,
For its opening up of the unimaginable,
Illuminating the heights and depths of existence,

Though damning me in the end.
But I would gladly pay that price.

The Curse of Caring

I cannot help myself;
I cannot cease to care.
I crave the simple life;
I desire normalcy,
But this passion,
This fire in my soul
For the vulnerable
You will not take from me.
You ignore my tears,
Refusing to answer me,
To put out the fire--
The fire burning in my soul.
Like Jonah I run.
I flee.
I hide myself away,
But you always find me,
And I return with the fire--
The fire burning in me
For the vulnerable.
And so must I bear the curse
The curse of caring
For the vulnerable.

The Funeral

The funeral - Joyce's...
Andreas didn't go.
He called it an act of freedom--
A stepping outside the Universal.
It was not original with him—
Not going to the funeral I mean.
L'Étranger was the influence,
Or I should say Meursault was.
Andreas found M's action intriguing.
Or maybe he was simply thinking
Of *let[ting] the dead bury the dead.*
In truth, he did not want the attention,
Being the oldest child and all.
In fact, it was not unlike
His accepting a childhood dare
To lie in the middle of the road,
Oncoming motor vehicles be damned.

The Divine Artist

Let us suppose, then,
that Art is living -
that the Artist's Creation
is dynamic, a living thing,
Shouldn't the Art, of necessity,
be allowed to self-evolve in its garden,
to freely take Its own course?
And Shouldn't They,
the Divine Artwork,
be free to explore Their Eden
without His micro-supervision,
His seeking to control the outcome?
And should He not
for both His New-born
provide a safe environment,
free from beguilement and subversion
and free from those wily creatures
who prey on the new-born?
And should He not also,
once His Art have reached maturity,
send them forth with His blessing
and with an open invitation
to return to their Eden at their pleasure?

Fairest Lord Jesus

And the virus roamed the land,
Filling hearts with anxiety and fear.
I ventured out into the noon day sun,
Pulling my scarf tightly around my neck
And tucking my chin into my collar
To avoid the unforgivingly cold wind.
I crossed over to the other side of the street.

Up ahead I saw several people standing in line.
A primary school was right there.
Were they waiting to pick of their children?
That couldn't be, for all the schools were closed.
I drew closer; the people were all elderly.
The line wound its way to the intersection
And disappeared around the corner.

Was the Catholic Church serving food?
That would be quite unusual.
Usually the elderly would go into the building,
And lunch would be given to them there.
Most of those standing in line wore face masks,
(As mandated by City authorities),
Some fully, others just under the nose.

As I got closer, the Church bell began to toll,
Playing a somber beat to my favorite hymn,

"Fairest Lord Jesus"
I turned the corner.
The line began at the church's side gate.
Some of the elderly stood shivering in the cold.
Faces read of frustration and hopelessness.

The bell continued tolling, "Fairest Lord Jesus."
The incongruity of the words of that hymn
And the scene before me was stark.
Inside the gate stood a table with food boxes.
And beside the table stood a fair "Lord Jesus" –
Mask on her face and gloves on her hands
To ensure she did not catch the deadly virus

The tolling continued: "Fairest Lord Jesus,"
A helper picked up a food box,
She handed it to the fair Jesus.
Then Jesus passed the box over the gate,
Making sure not to touch the recipient.
And I continued on my way
Singing the tune the church bell tolled:
"Je---sus is fai---rer,
Je---sus is pu---rer,
Who makes the woeful hea---rt to sing."

"But now that I have matured,
I have returned
to childlike thinking..."

"qui propter nos homines...descendit de caelis..."

I am the keeper of the gate -
Heaven's Gate -
And many souls have I seen
Who have this threshold crossed,
All making an entrance
But none an exit except that one time
When the One upon whose countenance
None dare gaze departed this Holy place.
A sad day it was when He sallied forth,
Intent on becoming the creature He created,
His heart set on one singular purpose -
"...nostra salutem..."

Resolute in His decision,
The Omnipotent Yahweh replied,
"Not by force but by love.
Not by force of arms

Or with chariots and horses
Will my creation be delivered
But by sacrifice, My sacrifice.
Only in my becoming one of them
Will their salvation be assured.
None but I will liberate them.

And so Heaven became silent.
Those whose voices day and night
Filled the air with songs of praise
To our Sovereign God
Now stood mute before His throne –
Before an empty throne.
For true love to any extreme would go.
He lay all on the line,
Everything.
Such did our Almighty,
Nothing held in reserve,
Going "all in,"
Risking all -
His deity, His sovereignty, His kingdom,
His very existence.
With nothing to fall back on -
No hybrid manifestation,
No both-God-and-man rationalization -

Risking all for every individual human,
Risking all for humankind.

As Jesus exited the gate that sad day,
He turned to me and said,
"I depart for earth this day to liberate man,
And to do so I must become man.
To become Man, I must give up my Deity.
In becoming human, I am affirming humanity,
Affirming my faith in humanity.
Be not afraid, all will be well."
With that he turned to go on His way
Then He turned to me once more
And with a chuckle said,
"It's funny - the irony...
A human saving fallen humanity."

And the Maker of humankind departed,
Leaving heaven and the world bereft
Of his almighty power and presence.
I am the keeper of the gate,
And, yes, I can attest that
For a brief while...
There was "no God."
He was busy being human

The Call

He sees it stretching forth, the weary land.
It bids him, "Come," with beckoning hand.
Should I heed, he wonders, and at what price?
Would I be willing to make the sacrifice?
Hesitant about pursuing a way he did not know,
He hears an assuring voice within, "Just go."

So off to that dry land the lonely traveler goes,
A promise of toil the only thing exposed.
And his question: Am I worthy of such a task?
Am I capable of doing that which is asked?
Welling up with tears and with the urge to cry,
He hears again that voice within, "Just try."

He surveys quietly the vast expanse,
Looking back wistfully upon all that chanced -
The travails he endured, the labors he wrought,
The triumphs he achieved, the battles fought.
Worn out and tired from all the work he'd done,
He hears once more, "Come, little one. Come."

The Empty Water Jar

I never dreamed that love
I would find on that sultry day
At that well near Sycharville
Where I first laid eyes on you.
A happy day it was for sure,
For love indeed I found.

As I watched you approach,
My weary feet ceased complaint,
And my tongue forgot its thirst.
And in that eternal moment,
That blazing orb in its zenith above
Relinquished its consuming power.

And how should I describe you
As you approached the well that day?
To say that you looked beautiful
Fails to give you your just due,
But to say, "A poem approached,"
Perhaps says more by far.

And when to the well you finally came,
You offered your smile as a gift,
And all I could muster in return,
Speechless and lost for words,
And with quivering, barely audible voice,

Was, "Will you give me a drink, please?"

That such a question I should ask
You found incredulous indeed,
For of different races were you and I,
With yours considered the lesser kind
And compounded by your sullied character
Which knowledge I acquired later.

In that moment love blossomed
Like a pair of lilies in the noonday sun.
And oblivious to the sweltering heat
We talked of my purpose and of our love.
Gone were my thirst and the tiredness in my feet
And your empty water jar forgotten.

And so love was in that instant born,
And that well became our rendezvous spot
Where at nights we would in secret meet,
Pouring out our love and desire each to each,
And heart to heart to one another speak,
While my followers lay in Sychar lost in sleep.

To save the many took second place;
In first place I gave your love full embrace.
My mission forgotten, by passion clouded,

Your bosom became my makura of roses,
Your lips my well-spring of refreshment,
And your love my source of nourishment.

And when in unguarded, thoughtless moments
My mind takes wandering flights of jealousy,
Wondering at the many lips that kissed you,
The hands that uncovered and caressed you,
And the many for whom your body you bared,
My joy is that your soul you bared to only me.

Contritum

Like curtains pulled apart,
The unforgiving darkness
Revealed a cold, grey dawn,
But no sweet serenade,
No fresh fragrance,
Nor colorful array
Hailed its appearance.
Only a sinister silence
Hung in that dead air,
Complemented by a creeping fog
Slithering its way among crooked trees,
Their life and that of the other inhabitants
Sucked out and rapaciously devoured
By the pitiless Swamp.
That habitation of the Son of the Morning,
Chief of that mighty horde
That waged ruthless battle
For dominion in the heavens,
The one who like lightening fell,
And like Sisyphus and Prometheus,
Eternally banished to absurdity.
In that deathly Swamp He roams,
Tormented by His schemes,
Plagued by His deeds,
The Tempter of Humanity's Son,
Destroyer of the children of Uzit,

Feared as well as hated,
The object of no one's love,
With heaven and earth
And the halls of justice,
Bearing witness against Him.
But how can any know
The anguished cry which
From that beleaguered soul doth rise
Day and night in that melancholy abode?
From the sacred text redacted
And by childish fables pushed out,
The story of that agonized and abandoned soul
Remains forever encrypted in that lonely place.
So amidst that dreary Swamp He wanders,
Bereft of His former splendor and glory,
Now of disrepute among men,
A mere mockery – the stuff of myth,
And with each passing day,
Passed over, forgotten,
Of far less significance than Father Noel,
Day after day uttering so plaintively,
Words enough to move the hardest heart,
Words of painful regret and sorrow,
"Forgive me;
Please forgive me."

Theologia Incarnationis

After the supper had ended
All the disciples sat in contemplation...

And Haysoos farted -
A long, loud fart,
And a severely odorous one too.

A nervous silence descended on the room.
Alarm gave place to amusement.

Andrew giggled
And ripped one too –
Almost as unpleasant as the one Haysoos blew.

All the others erupted in laughter.
And Haysoos joined in too.

Concluding Postscript to "*Eva ad rem*"

"We can't have it both ways.
Either Eve is entirely and solely culpable
Or the responsibility is fully mine."
Sabio

O Eva,
Dearest Eva,
Bearer of humanity's burden.
Poor Eva,
Our hapless Pandora,
Misogynized,
Maligned,
Misunderstood,
We pay homage to you;
We revere and honor you
And call you,
Mother.

Prelude to "The Letter"

And to think we had thought of...
We had thought of running away,
Running far, far away to a far-off place.
I was full of bliss at the thought.
He had come in and changed my life;
He had touched me like none other,
Reaching into the depths of my soul.
He talked of his mission, his purpose
He was destined for great things,
To accomplish great things.
He was a dreamer, with lofty dreams,
Dreams of bringing change,
Bringing to the poor, good news,
Bringing to the captives, release,
To the blind, sight,
To the oppressed, liberty...
Until I came into his life,
And we found in each other, love.
We talked of our lives together,
Many a night in our secret meeting place
Sharing kisses and warm embrace,
His head on my bosom,
Dreaming of our lives together,
Far removed from his mission,
Away from the burden of his followers.
For many a day my face was aglow,

My spirit radiant with joy,
For I was running away with my love.
And then came the day,
The day radiance gave place to gloom
And joy gave its lofty seat to sadness,
The day a little boy brought the letter,
The letter my love wrote to me
About his decision to face his destiny.
To drain the cup from which he must drink.

va-Bohu

Feelings of loneliness hound me.
Peerless and friendless am I
In this interminably tedious existence.
Blamed for everything,
Cannot do anything but good;
Cannot be anything but good,
For so am I infinitely hardwired.
I am not all powerful as is imagined
I am limited by my nature,
I cannot do evil; evil I cannot be.
It is not easy being me.
Do I envy those I brought into being?
Now that's a thought.
They have no fixed nature,
And can be whatever they desire –
Angels or brute beasts.
They can live,
Or they can choose not to live.
Maybe I do envy them
And long to be as they are.
I know not sleep, nor hunger.
I know not mirth, nor laughter.
I know nothing of erotic delight,
Neither know I pain or pleasure.
Who is more powerful, I or they?
Sometimes I am not so sure.

From Faith to Faith

I tried once, to become like them,
But failed miserably.
Like them I looked,
But my nature remained intact;
Theirs eluded me like the wind,
Mere anthropomorphic references -
The closest I can get to their nature.
I have learned, over time, to live
With being blamed for the destruction
And the suffering and death
Left in the wake of Nature's upheavals,
But far more hurtful is to be
Considered irrelevant,
To have my existence cast in doubt,
To be treated as though I am not,
And to be grossly misrepresented,
To be profoundly misunderstood
By those who profess to know me.
I can't continue further like this;
I can't bear this Eternal loneliness.
I want out, I want out,
But sadly, I can only live.

Prelude to the Journey Up the Mountain

"Art, not morality, is the truly essential metaphysical activity or pursuit of humanity."

--Friedrich Nietzsche

And must I blindly follow Your command,
Doing that most difficult thing You ask,
Raising the question whether a heart You own?
But no argument from me will You get,
For against You I am no match.
Yet I rebel, not in refusal, but in acquiescence.
For in so doing I rise above You in morality.
No cause for worry is mine, no feeling of guilt,
Since Heaven's endorsement have I acquired,
While Hell looks on gleeful, encouraging,
Mocking, awaiting the completion of the act.

How can I that dreaded night forget
When from You the words I received -
Fatal and murderous words none should hear -
A father's peace shattering,
The order of things disturbing.
Well that night I do remember
When at hearing those words
Heaven and earth hurled forth their protest,
Thundering and quaking their displeasure,
Bewailing Your abuse of power.

Later that night I watched him as he slept,
My only son –
My son, to whom I gave life.
I watched him as he slept,
Totally oblivious of the Divine plot,
Unmindful of the Despot's pleasure,
His life soon to be snuffed out, snatched away,
His life a mere gambling chip to test my faith,
A test of where my true love and fidelity lie.

From fitful sleep that solemn morn I rose,
Lonely and friendless, aged and wiser,
But with a heart of stone.
Of that which I was asked to do,
I could not speak.
Of that which I was about to do,
Neither friends nor wife could be privy,
For they would have considered me mad,
Numbered among those
From whom reason had taken flight,
And to be examined, put away, confined.

But far hence and in many places
Fools will analyze the event,
Expound upon the ordeal,
And marvel at the outcome,

Deeming me praiseworthy.
Those guided by faith will laud my faith,
Holding me up as witness and model.
And I am left with the nagging thought...
That I should have stood up to the Tyrant,
That I should have said, "No!"

But ask any child – two, three, four, or five…
Whether such a charge his endorsement has,
Whether such an instruction she would follow.
Note the resounding, "No!"
Note the incredulity of response
That such dictate from Him would come
And call into question His goodness.

But why listen to a child?
What does a child know?
And so, up to the mountain I will go,
There to confute existence,
To obliterate innocence,
To affirm the Unjust,
And to dare to confront the universe.

The Evidence of Things Not Seen

Into that place,
Where transcendence meets imminence,
They went –
Mother and child,
She, purposeful,
He, hesitant, diffident, timid.

In that place
Where stained-glass windows tell stories
And sculptures with wistful gaze
Look down upon votaries,
They stood –
Child and mother,
Embraced by the silence,
Awed by the holy -
That place of last resort
After all else fails.

In that place,
They knelt, side by side,
Mother and child.
No chance visit this,
But by maternal love propelled,
A mother's desperate heart
Pours out words unspoken
While Saint Peter, a child in his arm

And another at his side
Looks down upon them with sightless eyes.
Were those sightless eyes
Capable of sight
They would see
The boy's adoring and trusting gaze.
But who could know
Those words of sacred whispers
That from that child flowed?
Who could know the pain,
The torment,
The nights of restless sleep?
Who could know that mother's anguish
While, daily and helplessly,
Upon her suffering child she looks?
The "burnt offering" is made,
Dropped into the little box by the boy.
A mere penny,
Like the widow's mite,
But a sweet fragrance.

From that place,
That place of hope,
They went,
Hand in hand,
Child and mother,

Anticipating,
Expecting,
Believing.

Iostorum et Probum

No one considered us
(Or so it seemed),
As if we didn't exist -
Erased or omitted from their story,
Either way, obliterated,
Buried among the rubble
Of our beloved city,
Interred into the ground
By a precipitation
Of rocks, sulphur, and fire,
Victims of heaven's wrath,
The falling metals of destruction.
Our voices stilled, silenced.
Nour, Fatima, Osama, Ahmad,
Mahmoud, Yasmeen, Shaimaa',
And all the others -
The babes, the toddlers,
The pre-teens, the teens,
Children and grand-children -
Gone and unmentioned,
Not counted among the righteous
We suppose,
Since within our beautiful city,
Now synonymous with everything vile,
A place abhorred and disdained,
A place abhorred and disdained,

Not even ten were found.
Without ceremony,
Prematurely dispatched
In our youth's prime -
One while at chore
Another while at a mother's breast,
One while at study,
Some while at play,
Many while at sleep,
All, mere collateral,
Unimportant, unworthy of mention,
And of no significance
We suppose,
All lumped together
With the unrighteous.

O besieged Strip,
O beloved City,
Your destruction sought
Because of the outcry against you,
Victim of relentless bombardment.
In muted silence
Our voices rise
From your smoldering ashes
And from the collective consciousness,
Speaking loudly without reproof

And without condemnation or rebuke.
Ah, dear Strip, none hears us,
For we are but children,
Expendable and invisible
We suppose,
Unnecessary in the grand scheme,
Like insects exterminated,
Passed over,
Forgotten.

Some Crazy Guy in the Temple Courts

Wife: Honey, you are home early.

Husband: Yea

[Silence]

Wife: Is everything okay?

Husband: Everything is fine.

Wife: You don't look fine. What happened to your face? You are bleeding.

Husband: It's nothing.

Wife: Come. Let me take a look at it, love. Oh my! That's a deep gash you have there. What happened?

[Two children come running into the house. They see their mom attending to their dad]

Boy: Mom, what happened to Dad?

Wife: Take your sister, and go next door to Auntie.

Boy: But, Mom....

Wife: Don't 'But Mom' me. Go!

Boy: Okay.

Wife: Andreas, please tell me what happened.

Husband: A man came into the temple court with a whip and started yelling and turning over tables and beating us. There was pandemonium everywhere. People and cows, and goats, and sheep were running all over the place....Ow!!! That hurts.

Wife: Sorry, love.

Husband: People were falling all over each other. I got caught above my eyebrow with one of the cords of his whip. I fell to the ground instantly. I believe I blacked out for a moment. But I got up and managed to get out of there very quickly. I saw this guy who had a huge welt on his naked back. He was just lying there...This really hurts. Is it still bleeding? He might have also been hurt in the stampede.

Wife: Were you able to sell the goats?

Husband: No, I wasn't. All seven of them got lost in the fracas. I looked all over, but I couldn't find them.

Wife: Oh no! What are we going to do? Leaving Shitim and going all the way up to Jerusalem for nothing? How are we going to make out? And the man. Who was he anyway? Just like that? What kind of madman will attack people like that? But I am so glad you are safe. I am tired of the violence in this land. But I am glad you are safe. Let me get you something to eat. We don't have much today.

Chatting With My Father

Remember when I used to be afraid of You?
Now I am not afraid of You anymore.
I mean no disrespect when I say that.
I acknowledge Your matchless power...
That You can obliterate me in a heartbeat.
So, knowing that such is the case,
Why should I be afraid of You?
But I do hold You in the highest regard.

[Pardon me if I use the lower case henceforth.
I mean no disrespect.
It is less tedious is all.]

I certainly accept that your Book is your Word.
Some of the things you say therein I accept
And surely do appreciate.
There are some things, however,
That I find nauseating,
And some things I find hard to take seriously.

Sometimes the book portrays you as a caring,
Sometimes merciful and benevolent,
And sometimes you come across as childish.
And I might add...
A hardass,
Kinda petty,
Petulant,

Egoistic,
Egotistic,
Brutal,
Cruel.
You are on record of ordering genocide –
Slaughtering entire peoples,
Including women and children.
And seriously?
You get angry over wooden and stone gods?
Because some people prefer those over you?
And killing them on those accounts?

And you know what I fail to comprehend?
Your system of punishment.
You created us to be free,
And yet you punish us when we act freely.
And this whole business about being damned
Simply for not accepting the Nazarene...
It's a bit over the top...don't you think?

And how about a template for living?
You provided us with none at birth,
Leaving us victims to many competing scripts
And not knowing for sure which one is true.
And frankly,
Regarding your promise of Heaven...

It does not appeal to me.
Milk and honey do not appeal to me,
Neither do pearly gates and streets of gold.
Just put me in a forest with my favorite book,
And I am good.
No, not the Bible, the book Ganesha wrote.
And to be quite honest with you,
I have absolutely no interest in living eternally.
Don't get me wrong...
I truly love and enjoy my human experience,
But after it is over, I prefer to return to all things.

I was talking to a friend the other day,
And your name came up...
About what happened in Eden.
I told her that as far as parenting goes
You are not my role model.
Think about what you did to mama Eve
And what you did to papa Adam for example:
What parent would do that to her kids,
Putting them in harm's way like you did,
In the situation in which you put Mama Eve?

Sorry, that's my grandchild calling. Gotta go.

A Declaration of Hope

The New Year appeared suddenly,
Holding tenuously in its turbulent wake
Ever disappearing and aborted promises,
Empty resolutions already forgotten.
The pain, my constant companion,
Etched its unseen marks mercilessly,
Reawakening feelings of resentment,
Nurturing hopelessness and hatred,
Leaving in its trail a dull, pounding apathy.
Languishing aspirations lie in the dust,
Ground underfoot and discarded,
Onerous to bear in the desolate void -
Diagnosis feeding deathly despair.
In the languid, littered streets below
Sated revelers reluctantly slink away,
Mere silhouettes and echoes of being,
Yesterday's dewdrops dried up by the sun,
Refusing to accept vaporous impermanence.
Evaporated dreams and futile longing merge,
Forming an impregnable alliance,
Unseating vain hope and eroding certainty,
Giving the scepter to the dreaded malady.
Emptied of hope, this tyrant I embraced,
Accepting the inevitable, waving the flag.
No negotiation necessary, for by pain coerced,
Defeated, once the news was first received.

Misty-eyed, I gaze wistfully out the window,
Yearning for significance, slithery and elusive,
Searching for some vindication for existence.
Then I saw myself at the platform's edge,
Recalling the little girl looking softly at me,
Entreating me tenderly with her soft, black eyes.
No words, but her eyes said it: "Please…Don't!"
Gazing out the window, I survey the silence,
Taking no notice of the pain's pitiless onslaught,
Holding on, holding on, though by a thread,

…to one singular thought…
…to one hope…

"The Eternal God is my Refuge and my Strength."

“God,...please come back.”

“Mommy!
Daddy seh there is no God, Mommy.
Why God go away, Mommy?
Don’t He like we anymore?
An’ did He tek gentle Jesus wid Him,
An’ di Holy Spirit,
An’ Hail Mary full of grace?
An’ did Allah go way wid Him too, Mommy,
An’ prophet Muhammad
(Peace be upon him),
An’ Lord Vishnu,
An’ Lord Krishna,
An’ Lord Indra?
Will there be church no mo’e,
Or temple,
Or mosque, Mommy?
An’, Mommy,
Who is gwine pray for us sinners,
Now and at the hour of our death, Amen
If Hail Mary full of grace gone too?
Did God leave because I is a bad boy, Mommy?”

Mommy is listening to soap opera on the radio.
“Boy, leave me alone.
Can’t you see I busy?”

A little later we see the little boy, barefeet,
Wearing only a pair of short khaki pants
With torn back side revealing his butt cheeks.
He is kneeling on the ground beside a tree—
A jamoon tree.

"Shhhhh...
He is praying...
Let's listen in..."

"God, please don' go way.
Please come back.
Please, please...
Ah promise I is going to be a good boy,
And ah will tell my friends,
All a dem,
To be good boys too.
And please bring back Holy Mother Mary
So she can pray for us sinners,
Now and at the hour of our death, Amen.
An' don't forget to bring back my hero,
My favorite,
My Gentle-Jesus-meek-and-mild-
Look-upon-this-little-child,
An' di Holy Spirit,
An' Allah,

An' prophet Muhammad
(On whom be peace),
An' Lord Vishnu,
An' Lord Krishna,
An' Lord Indra
So we can go to church,
An' go to temple,
An' go to mosque again.
Amen."

"Mommy, Mommy!
Look, Mommy!
A rainbow! A rainbow!
That means God come back!
He answer mi prayer, Mommy!

"Daddy, Daddy!
God come back!
He come back!
Come see di rainbow, Daddy!
Di rainbow mean He come back."

"Hell, no!"

And that was Sara's response.
Believe me.
I was not at all surprised by it.
"Hell no! Not my son,"
She continued,
Even more emphatically.
"How dare He command such?"
"Has He ever given birth?
Does he know what it means?
What Motherhood means?
Does He have a clue?
How dare He!?
I don't care how all powerful He is.
I respect His power,
But I am not afraid of Him.
And how dare you!"
I hadn't planned on telling her,
But I felt I had to.
What do I do now?
Shall I proceed up that mountain?
Truth be told,
I would rather face His wrath
Than face my wife's wrath.
What do I do now?
Any ideas?

The Last Homily

Andreas Pistis agonized over his sermon.
What should he say to the congregation?
How can he preach to them of faith,
In particular, of Abraham's faith?

Interrupting his Gethsemane moment,
His daughter barged into the room.
Her cousin followed after.
They were playing hide-and-seek.

"Kara-Joi, I have a question for you."
"But daddy, Anthony and I are playing."
"It will take only a moment.
Please...This is very important."

She conferred with Anthony.
"Okay daddy, what is the question?"
"If you had a son, and God told you...
If God told you to...."

He paused, as if searching for the words.
"If God told me what, daddy?"
"If God told you to kill your son,
What would you do?"

"God would never ask that of anyone.

That would not be God speaking.
That would be the Devil speaking."
Sucking her teeth, she walked out of the room.

As he stood before the congregation,
And as he brought his sermon to a close,
He said, "Ladies and gentlemen,
I do not have the faith of Abraham.

If God asked me to kill my son, Carlos,
I could not carry out His command.
I would tell him the truth; I would say to Him,
"Father, I love my son more than I love You."

May God grant us the strength
To have the faith of Abraham. Amen

The Least of These

It emanated from her
Like crooked tendrils–
The Stench.
It clung to us in desperation,
Pleadingly craving our attention,
And like a parasite,
Grabbing onto our garments,
Winding its way around our bodies,
And reaching into our pores and nostrils
As if seeking escape from its source,
From the poor and pitiful creature
From whom it originated.
We who sat near her,
Once we realized
From whence the smell came,
We took flight...in desperation...
And even after fleeing
That mass of human stench,
That none too pleasant fragrance
Stayed with us,
Itself begging to be far removed
From that bundle of putrid degradation,
This bipedal ferment
Of urine and fecal matter,
Heaven's dearest,
God's "least of these."

But what we did not see
Was the little child,
The child who with her mother,
Stayed in the car,
Unmindful of the stench,
Unmindful of the bipedal ferment
Of urine and fecal matter,
The child who,
With a doll cradled in her arm
And leaving her mother's side
And ignoring her protestation,
Walked over to the woman and said,
"Do you want to play with me?
To play with my doll and me?"

"Spare some tears,...please."

The Shadows cast their brilliance
On wet and littered streets
Where dreams are trampled
By a dazed and dying multitude
Unmindful of the teary-eyed supplication
From an ***of-such-is-the-kingdom-of-heaven***
Holding forth an inane paper cup
Like an ignored and rejected prayer.

Even the sultry light retreated
From this disparate apparition,
Earnestly withholding its life,
Reserving it for an echoic new day,
Leaving the mendicant little seeress
To grope about for significance,
A lost and weeping child
Looking for the Way that leads nowhere.

And still she persists, this prophetess,
Hapless victim of a ***dare*** long ago,
Salvaging dreams from trashcans.
And yet she persists, our little sage,
Pleading with the surging crowd,
"Spare some change, spare some change,"
But the dead multitude moves on -
Like routed clouds, uneasy, discomfited.

Subdued reminiscences and stolen desires
Weave their way along broken sidewalks
And among wistful, shadowy figures
Suppressing fleeting dreams of yesterday
While our threadbare, bare-footed Sybil,
Her sole possessions in a shopping cart,
Divine of the Wrath to come, pleading,
"Spare some change, spare some change.

Now change there is in abundance,
But of compassion there is a dearth,
For with parched and barren hearts
A legion of dried-up eyes stare,
Sightless, seeing but not seeing,
While passing judgement on the malodorous,
Tispossessed child, too early an adult,
As she pleads,
"Please,...spare some tears.
Spare some tears,... please."

"Sickness, A Curse"

Eager with anticipation,
A recent convert to the Faith
Young and on fire for "the Lord,"
Anticipating the casting out,
Casting out of a "demon"
(I found out years later it had a name—
Cerebral palsy).
Converging on the place
With a group of fellow believers,
Freddie our leader,
The charismatic Freddie,
The "sickness is curse" Freddie.
We never got the demon out,
A lack of faith according to Freddie,
Not a lack of his faith, mind you.
Ours, the rest of us in the group.
I never forgot that evening,
Well not so much the evening
But the possesee,
Her body severely contorted,
Her tongue twisted in her mouth,
Preventing speech
And producing only moans.
The more we shouted,
"In Jesus name,"
The more agitated she became,

Which agitation Freddie attributed to…
You guessed it…
The demon.
I recall while joining in the
"In Jesus name,"
Observing the entire event…
Meta cognitively.
You'll have to look up the term.
I do not feel like explaining it here.
Anyway…
If God declares sickness a curse,
He'll receive no argument from me,
But that millstone around my neck
I refuse to wear.
My starting point is:
"I am fearfully and wonderfully made,"
And that wonderful are His works,
Which works include the human body
And it incomprehensible immune system,
Engendering inconclusive debate
Between Pasteur and Bechamp
And terrain theory and germ theory.
And so I celebrate my body,
Exceedingly happy with its finiteness,
Celebrating its inexplicable cycle -
From beginning to end

From Faith to Faith

And watching the intrigue
Of the body's development to breakdown,
With pain as the undercurrent of both
Like the hammering and sawing
Applied to a new house in construction
And the leaks and peeling paint
Of said house in deterioration -
Celebrating death as equally as birth
And refusing to accept death as curse,
But eagerly looking to meet it head on,
To return to all things,
To fall into my eternal sleep.
But I digress....

And the same with my body,
Assailed (so it seems)
With that which we call "sickness,"
The flu, headaches, cancer, and others,
The likes of which,
If and when they appear,
I deem my visitors to whom I play host,
"...serving tea to friends" -
If I may take a line from Eliot's
"Portrait of a Lady" -
Allowing their stay for as long as they wish
And saying little about their presence

To those who care about me or call me friend
As their focus seem more on the desire
To know the name of a particular friend
And making qualitative distinction among them
As indicated by the level of alarm generated,
Not realizing that no qualitative difference
Is indicated among "sickness."
And so hung up on naming the "sickness"
And so alarmed by its perceived severity,
They lose sight of the most important thing,
Glorifying the Eternal God -
Our Refuge and our Strength.
And so I seek not or desire "prayers"
For my body's healing
Or for my visitors' departure
But simply allow the inconvenience
And much to my own profit.
For in my glorying in the inconvenience
(Of hosting my visitors)
I develop patience,
Which in turn produces character,
The logical corollary of which is hope,
Which makes me impervious to shame
Because God's love permeates my being.

Further, if it is the case that

"In Him I live and move and have my being,"
Then that which "happens to me"
Happens to Him…
Which means nothing "happens to" me.
And I do not consider it strange
Concerning my "visitations"
As though something strange
"Happened to [me]."
I used to say to my children,
"Nothing can happen to you
When you are with your daddy."
And nothing can "happen to" me
When I am in my Eternal Daddy."
And so,
"I shall sit here, serving tea to [my] friends,"
To the new ones who might show up
And to those few perpetually here with me,
Including the importunate one
I recently took to the ER for care.

And concerning the woman,
The "demon possessed" woman,
I carry her with me still,
In my heart,
And from time to time I say to her,
"I am sorry."

A Little-Known Secret

The pain was unbearable.
I could not go on.
The tears broke the dam of my will,
Pouring forth
And running down my cheeks.

Three children stood ten meters ahead,
Dressed for school,
Waiting for transportation perhaps.
Two boys and a girl,
Ages eleven to twelve I supposed.

An idea formed in my mind.
I was desperate.
I greeted them as I drew closer,
Grimacing in pain.
In unison, they responded,
"Good morning, Uncle."
They listened to my plea for help,
Their faces expressionless
Yet attentive and engaging
My being a stranger notwithstanding.

I made my request
And gave a brief rationale for making it.
They looked at each other,

Surprise and empathy in their eyes
And an unspoken agreement
About the next step.
The girl suggested that they join hands,
Inviting me to do the same with them.
The details of her petition I cannot recall,
For many years have since passed,
But I do recall that the pain stopped.
This was not too long after leaving them.
I recalled also that as I turned to leave
One of the boys asked,
"Uncle, is it true?"
"Is what true, son?"
"Is it true what you told us?
That God listens to children
More than he listens to grownups?"
"Indeed it is, son,; it is.
In fact, only children are accepted in Heaven."
"Then, Uncle, if that is the case
Why should I want to become an adult?"
"Ah, son.
By all means become an adult.
It is part of our existence cycle;
But always remain a child at heart."
And with a smile the old man turned
And continued on his journey.

From Faith to Faith

"Except you…become as little children,
you shall not enter into the kingdom of heaven."
Matthew 18:3
Father Ionnes,
I will never forget a certain night
When upon hearing that blessed hymn,
"Just as I am without one plea…,"
I embraced our Lord and Savior,
And with a rugged determination,
A ruthless commitment,
And a reckless abandonment
Embarked on an unforgettable journey—
A journey of self-discovery
And of the knowledge of my Father.
But as to the origin of my faith odyssey
I cannot count that seminal moment.
What was the starting point?
My awaking to consciousness as an infant.
At that awakening I saw two individuals.
They were the first persons I saw--
A man and a woman.
I formed the notion that they were God,
My "Ground of Being,"
Especially the man

Then they took me to school.

In fact, the woman did,
For the man had to work.
To my utter confusion,
The man and woman deferred to my teacher.
The teacher also beat me like they did.
Her having that freedom
Plus their deference to her
Meant she was indubitably God.

Soon the deity passed to Father Singh
He lived in the place with the icons,
The place with the stained-glass windows,
The place in which you only whisper.
The man and woman went there
(Only on Sundays),
Taking me with them.
Father Singh called them up and fed them,
Putting little white things in their mouths
And saying, "The Body of Christ,"
To which they replied, "Amen."

Further confusing me,
I heard Father Singh talking to "God."
I thought he was God!
I soon found out there were three of them--
God the Father,

God the Son,
And God the Holy Ghost.
That last one confused me
As I was scared of ghosts.
Anyway, I realized Father Singh was not God.

Then I saw photos of God the Son.
He had blonde hair and blue eyes,
And he was white,
With his heart outside on his chest.
They called it the sacred heart of Jesus.
I saw no photos of the other two Gods.
God the Son was cool.
I read a lot of nice things about him
And about how he did lots of miracles.
My favorite was the bread and two fish.
He fed five thousand people with those.
I found that so amazing!!
I didn't like that they crucified him though,
But I was very happy when he resurrected.
We he like a ghost or something?
That was always my question.

And then I found out about Muhammed--
On whom be peace.
You are supposed to say,

"On whom be peace"
He was not God;
He was a prophet.
Allah is God.
I learned to say:
La ilaha illallah,
Muhammadur Rasulullah
It means:
"There is no God but Allah,
And Muhammad is His Prophet."
"Please teach my son about Islam,"
That was what my dad said to the Imam.
I attended Maktab on weekdays,
Mosque for prayers on Fridays,
Mass on early Sunday morning,
Sunday school at the clap-hand church,
Bible class on Wednesdays,
And the Hindu temple on Thursdays.
I never missed attending any of them.
And I kept all my Sunday school tracts,
With the wonderful Jesus stories
And the beautiful color pictures.

Going to the Hindu temple was my favorite
The sounds of the flute and tabla captivated me.
And the sweet smell of incense

And the stories from the *Mahabharata*—
About Krishna's conversation with Arjuna,
About Bishma, Karna, Kuntu and many others.
I could listen to those stories all day.
And the stories from the *Holy Bible* too.
The *Holy Koran* was not so much fun.
It did not have any fun stories.
And if I got shipwrecked on a desert island
And I had to choose one book to take with me,
I would take the Mahabharata.

Were God, Allah, and Krishna different Gods?
That question never crossed my mind.
They all seemed one and the same to me.
I didn't like God and Allah so much.
They seemed mean.
Krishna and his many selves I liked.
They seemed more human.
But my Hero was Jesus.
He is the greatest hero of all heroes.
Because he left Heaven to become a man.
He became a man to liberate mankind.

Eventually I grew up.
I became a man, an adult,
And when I became a man,

"I put away the thinking of a child,"
"I put away childlike things."
I questioned everything,
Doubted everything,
Rejected everything,
Debated everything—
Source theories,
Atonement theories,
Theodicy,
The Trinity,
Theological frameworks,
Christology,
Soteriology,
Free will,
Determinism,
Biblical literalism,
Interpretative theories...
And the list goes on and on...
My knowledge of everything, I increased,
And the more I increased my knowledge,
The more impoverished became my knowledge.
The more magnified became my ignorance.

Then the realization struck me....
A sort of epiphany--
That my most authentic religious experience,

My most authentic faith experience,
Was not the faith experience of my adult years,
Which years, I am proud to say,
Never saw me questioning God's existence,
Or the substitutionary sacrifice of Jesus,
Or the infallibility of the Word,
Or disrespecting my Father in any way.
No! Not by any means.
My attitude was always that of
Fear and trembling...
But I digress.
And so...
My most authentic experience?
It was the faith experience of my childhood.
And with that realization,
Putting away my adult thinking
With all its skepticism and rationalism
I returned to childlike things
To my childlike thinking,
To childlike innocence,
And that has made all the difference.

POSTSCRIPT

The Floating Log

The inevitable --
It looms large on the horizon,
Getting ominously closer.
Time was when it was merely a thought,
Like waiting at the end
Of an interminable line
And with endless time to spare.
Or so I thought - fool that I was
By such an illusion to be ensnared.
For now that Silent One
Inches mockingly closer
With every wrinkle on the skin,
Every sudden loss of balance,
Every blurred vision,
Every moment of forgetfulness,
Every unbuttoned fly.
Slowly and slowly do those rotted logs
Drift along -
Drifting, drifting, drifting -
Until deposited upon the shore of oblivion.
And so, the names are called,
Those up ahead as well as those behind,
Without regard for who came first.
But the line moves forward.

In the meanwhile we become preoccupied.
We occupy ourselves with vain pursuits,
Ignoring the unalterable,
Disregarding the unavoidable,
Until like Brian's fruit we fall,
Briefly remembered and talked about
But then soon forgotten.
But what does being talked about matter?
Of what import is being remembered
When I shall be in eternal sleep?
Absolutely nothing.
But my mind is set,
Just a few more ahead of me.
I shall not wait around to be fussed over
Or mark time lying in some bed,
But I shall pack my warashee
And head off into the woods -
To my favorite spot in the woods -
There to wait my turn,
To wait my call,
The inevitable name-call -
"Andreas?
Andreas Pistis?"
Like it was for Rema and for Morro -
The call to return to all things,
To rest my tired soul in eternal sleep...
To return to nothingness, blissfully sweet.

From Faith to Faith

www.ingramcontent.com/pod-product-compliance
Lightning Source LLC
LaVergne TN
LVHW090605110826
845146LV00001B/265

* 9 7 9 8 2 3 4 0 5 2 5 1 3 *